# CHESTERTON

## As Seen by His Contemporaries

G. K. C.
Done especially for this book
by
CONRADO W. MASSAGUER

# CHESTERTON

## As Seen by His Contemporaries

CYRIL CLEMENS

Author of

"MY COUSIN MARK TWAIN,"

Etc.

With Introduction by

### E. C. BENTLEY

Author of

"TRENT'S LAST CASE,"

Etc.

**HASKELL HOUSE PUBLISHERS** LTD.

*Publishers of Scarce Scholarly Books*

NEW YORK. N. Y. 10012

**1969**

First Published 1939


HASKELL HOUSE PUBLISHERS Ltd.
*Publishers of Scarce Scholarly Books*
280 LAFAYETTE STREET
NEW YORK, N. Y. 10012




Library of Congress Catalog Card Number: **76-92958**




**Standard Book Number 8383-0968-2**




Printed in the United States of America

DEDICATED
with his kind permission
to
BENITO MUSSOLINI
a warm admirer of Chesterton
and his work.

# TABLE OF CONTENTS

Introduction ........ by E. C. Bentley
Chapters
One ................ Boyhood Days
Two ........ Literary Apprenticeship
Three ........ Meetings with G. K. C.
Four ................ Some Friends
Five ........ On the English Platform
Six ....... On the American Platform
Seven...Some Recollections of G. K. C.
Eight.......Chesterton at New Haven
Nine ................ At Notre Dame
Ten.Chesterton and American Authors
Eleven.The Author Visits Top Meadow
Twelve .............. Father Brown
Thirteen ........... Some Appraisals
Fourteen ................. The Poet
Fifteen ......... Chesterton the Man

# INTRODUCTION
## by E. C. Bentley

———

Mr. Cyril Clemens' book about Gilbert Chesterton is of an unusual and, to my taste, a deeply interesting sort. Some one has remarked that the most satisfactory biographies were those in which the letters and journals of the subject bulked largest, since these, telling their own tale, showed the man better than any biographer could do it. Mr. Clemens has assembled a vast number of other people's memories and appreciations of G. K. C.; and it may be said that they show the attitude of his contemporaries towards him better than any individual critic could describe it.

There is a remarkable note of unanmity in these personal recollections and judgments. There are differences of view about the value of G. K. C.'s work; about the relative importance of this or that of its many aspects; about his matter or style in lecturing; about the quality of his wit, and many points more. But as to the nature of the man as he was there is hardly any difference at all. He won the hearts of those who met him because of his manifest goodness of heart and happiness of temper; these things were as apparent to all who came near him as was his physical being.

I do not imagine that Mr. Clemens asked me to write this introduction with the idea of my setting forth any opinions about the place of G. K. C. in our literature. I could offer none of any critical value, because for me the man and his work have always been one, and I have been for most of my life intensely prejudiced in favour of the man. Mr. Clemens knew of me, I suppose, as a boyhood friend of G. K. C. —as I appear in his Autobiography— and perhaps as having dedicated a book of mine to him in terms which told some fraction of what my feeling towards him was. I may, then, say now that I first met him at that time of life when personal influence counts for

11

most, and one's nature is in the making for good or evil. His friendship was the best thing that ever happened to me, and I have always thanked God for it.

Essential goodness, perfect sincerity, chivalrous generosity, boundless good-temper, a total absence of self-esteem —these are lovable traits; and with them, even in boyhood, were united brilliant intellectual powers and an enormous gift of humor. The effect of it all on an impressionable youth of fifteen or so can perhaps be guessed. For years we were as near to each other as it is possible for friends to be, I think; but there was no one who knew him even slightly that did not feel something of the spiritual attraction that he exercised—always in utter unconsciousness of it.

G. K. C. was too conspicuously unlike the ordinary boy to be popular, in the sense of being on the best of terms with all and sundry. He was without any desire to excel or take the lead in any direction. He was unconscious of the very existence of games. He was

III

steeped in literature and art; and he could, at need, be perfectly happy with his own thoughts and the fruits of his imagination. He was, on the other

hand, not unpopular; it was impossible for even an ill-natured boy, I should think, to dislike him; but his circle of friends was small in those early days. I have written something about this time of our lives to Mr. Clemens who has quoted it at the outset of this book. What I have been saying in this place is an attempt to express what Gilbert Chesterton meant to me.

That circle of friends which was so small was to become as wide as any man's of our time, as the recognition of his genius increased, and the magic of his personality gained greater scope. No death can ever have been mourned with a deeper sincerity of personal affection by so many, in his own country and in others.

IV

# CHAPTER ONE

## BOYHOOD DAYS

One of Chesterton's earliest and staunchest friends, Mr. E. C. Bentley, recalls,

"Chesterton was in his schooldays the centre of a small group of boys. They formed a club under his chairmanship . . . the Junior Debating Club, so called to distinguish it from the School Union Society, which was the preserve of the senior boys. He never did, as he states in his memoirs, any work at school in the academic sense, and so never rose to the position of a star boy. The star boys did not understand him and classed him as a freak who was unlikely to do the school any credit. He was so exceptionally untidy and absent-minded, even at the age when the ordinary boy becomes careful of his appearance, that he did not fit into the picture at all; and it needed the insight of Walker, the High Master of his day, to divine that there was the stuff of genius in him, and to ordain (as G. K. tells in his own modest way) that on the strength of a remarkable prize poem . . . the only 'regular' thing

he ever did at school . . . he should
'rank with the eighth form,' the highest, to which he would never have attained on his school performance. Very
few of the boys of whom he saw most
did anything in the field of letters in
after life." The poet Edward Thomas
was not at St. Paul's with G. K. C. as
many think. Mr. Robert Eckert, the biographer of Thomas, states that the
latter was a schoolmate of Cecil,
G. K. C.'s younger brother.

Mr. Bentley continues: "About
G. K. C.:—His spare time at school—
which, as he makes clear in his Autobiography, was mostly spent . . . . I
should say entirely . . . in talking, reading, writing, and drawing pictures. He
had a wonderful decorative handwriting, and was already a masterly
draughtsman. Apart from walking, of
which he never tired as a boy, he took
no part in any sport. His sight was
always very bad without his glasses.
He was nevertheless strong and healthy
as a boy, rather slim than otherwise; it
was not until the twenties that he began to put on flesh. It was not ordinary fatness; I believe some gland trouble must have been at the root of it.

"Speaking generally, Chesterton would
talk about everything when at school
that had to do with the realm of ideas.
He never took much interest in things

that are called practical. Politics in a broad sense he would talk about, but for the details of legislation he cared nothing. He always was, of course, what we know as a Liberal; in the large sense he remained a Liberal all his days.

"Literature he would discuss by the hour, especially poetry. He hated the fashionable decadence of that time . . . say 1890—1900 . . . as may be seen from the dedication to 'The Man Who Was Thursday.' He delighted in pictorial art, above all in the generous idealism of G. F. Watts.

"As to books, G. K. C. never gave any attention to those which constituted school-work. He was passionately fond of Scott and of course, Dickens. He knew Tennyson, Browning, Swinburne by heart, and had enjoyed every other English poet in large degree. He did not care in those days for lighter reading.

"There was a school library, but it was reserved for the use of the highest class in the school, which G. K. C. never attained. There was a popular fiction library also, but he did not, I think, make use of it. G. K. C. was too amiable to get into fights, but he would use his strength occasionally in standing between a small boy and others who were badgering him. He honored religion,

3

but had none whatever of a doctrinal kind until years later."

"Chesterton, as I knew him in 1889," writes Mr. E. W. Fordham, another old schoolmate, "was utterly unlike the average English schoolboy. He took no part in games. He showed no particular brilliance as a scholar, and yet far from being looked down upon, he was, I think, always regarded as one who lived in a different mental world from the rest of us, a world that many of us admired from afar but would never expect, or, it may be, ever hope to enter. We felt, though we never alluded to, his mental pre-eminence. Thus when the Junior Debating Club was formed, G. K. became Chairman without question and without a rival. It was obvious that he alone was fitted for the post, and most admirably he filled it. The teas at the houses of the various members of the Club which preceded the debates were often tempestuous to the last degree, but Gilbert, although he took no share in the more physical aspects of our revelry, was very far from playing the part of a wet blanket.

"His laugh was the loudest and the most infectious of all. There were times when the boisterous manifestations of some of us overflowed into, and tended to overpower, the Debates. Then, with the utmost good temper, G. K.

4

would assert himself, and order would be restored.

"I remember once, after I myself had been particularly noisy and troublesome, Gilbert explained to me that the throwing of buns and slices of cake did not really help in the production of good debates, and he hinted, very kindly and seriously, that some restraining action might have to be taken if the rioting did not diminish. I hope, indeed, I believe, I took the hint. This occasion was thereafter referred to as the day 'when the Chairman spoke seriously to Mr. F.'

"G. K. was the mainspring of the Junior Debating Club. He was valiantly supported by Oldershaw, Bentley, and others, but without him neither the Club itself, nor that strange little magazine, 'The Debater' could have flourished as each of them did. Like boy, like man. That which he believed in he put his whole heart into, and never spared himself in furthering its interests. He gave the Junior Debating Club his eager and inspiring support for the two very good reasons, that it gave great enjoyment to himself and a few of his friends, and that he thought it a widening and humanizing influence —completely outside the range of ordinary school affairs. The Chairman loved the Junior Debating Club, and

5

most certainly the J. D. C. loved the Chairman.

Mr. Fordham pins further recollections around the "Autobiography":

"I am a prejudiced person. Fifty years of friendship and admiration are an insuperable bar to impartiality.

"G. K. C. and I were at school together: we were fellow members of the Junior Debating Club of which he was Chairman. We both contributed to our Club's magazine, 'The Debater.' I wrote rubbish; he wrote articles and verses of a very different quality. In this book he speaks almost with contempt of his 'juvenilia.' They were in fact such as very few boys of his age could have produced. Even then, at the age of fifteen or sixteen, he had a sense of style and a command of language which the High Master of St. Paul's and other authorities did not fail to recognize. 'The Dragon,' one article begins, 'the Dragon is the most cosmopolitan of impossibilities.'

"As I say, I admired Gilbert Chesterton throughout his life, and after reading his 'Autobiography' I admire him still more. My attitude is rather that of a hero-worshipper than a critic, but I believe that no impartial critic could read this book and fail to see that here was a genius, and better, a brave and an honest man, a man who loved life

6

and loved his friends, loved laughter and hated oppression; in short a very great man. Despite all the modesty with which it is written, the book makes all these things clear. From beginning to end it is a magnificent **apologia pro vita sua;** nevertheless I hope it will not be the sole record of his life. There are countless things that he could not and would not tell of himself but that should not be forgotten. 'Belloc,' he writes, 'still awaits a Boswell.' It is equally true that Chesterton awaits one. Is it legitimate to hope that his Boswell may be Belloc? There is a grand harvest to be gathered by his Boswell, whoever that may prove to be. G. K. C. was a brilliant talker. He banished dullness from whatever company he was in. No argument arose but he would drive home his point by some arresting illustration. We were arguing once as to whether some policy or other were good or bad. 'The word 'good,' said G. K., 'has many meanings. For example, if a man were to shoot his grandmother at a range of 500 yards I should call him a good shot, but not necessarily a good man.'

"No one could stump him by an unexpected question. He took part in a debate many years ago at, I think, the Lyceum Club, and in the course of his speech he discussed, as did other speak-

7

ers, various racial characteristics. After the debate I was walking round with him when an elderly lady whom he did not know came up and said with something of a simper, 'Mr. Chesterton, I wonder if you could tell what race I belong to?' With a characteristic adjustment of his glasses he replied at once, 'I should certainly say, Madam, one of the conquering races.'

"Only a year or two ago he watched with tolerant, and indeed highly vocal amusement, (his was both the strangest and the jolliest laugh man ever had) a representation of himself in some private theatricals. When they were over he said to the daughter of the player who had impersonated him—a sturdy figure, it is true, but less generously planned than the original — 'Do you know I believe your father is Gilbert Chesterton and I am only a padded impostor.'

"Reading this book has recalled these trifles to my mind just as it has recalled the figure of the boy Chesterton as I first knew him in the early nineties. I can see him now, very tall anl lanky, striding untidily along Kensington High Street, smiling and sometimes scowling as he talked to himself, apparently oblivious of everything he passed, but in reality a far closer observer than most, and one who not only observed but remembered what he had seen. The fascination of this book is, in great part, due to the fact that he retained these powers of observation and memory throughout his life, and that he has applied them to himself as rigorously and as vividly as to his fellows.

" 'I should thank God for my creation,' said Gilbert's grandfather, 'if I knew I was a lost soul.' Gilbert would have done the same. 'The primary problem for me,' he writes, 'was the problem of how men could be made to realize the wonder and splendour of being alive,' and it is because he himself did realize it that he is able to say of his later years, 'I have grown old without being bored. Existence is still a strange thing to me, and as a stranger I give it welcome.'

"Chesterton begins this book with a joke about his baptism. It is characteristic of the man. He loved laughter as much as he hated hypocrisy. 'I have never understood,' he says, 'why a solid argument is any less solid because you make the illustrations as entertaining as you can.' It is because, in this autobiography the philosophy is spiced with fun, and the fun sometimes spiced with philosophy, that so true a picture of the man emerges from the book. When he looks at himself he sees not only an intensely interesting being but

9

also an intensely amusing one. He
speaks of his school days as the period
during which 'I was being instructed
by somebody I did not know, about
something I did not want to know.' He
tells how on his wedding day he stopped
to buy a glass of milk at some haunt of
his infancy, and again to buy a revolver
and cartridges 'with a general notion
of protecting my bride from the pirates
doubtless infesting the Norfolk Broads.'

"You will find the same amusement he
found if you read and re-read his chapter on 'Friendship and Foolery,' his story
of the sudden invasion of Henry James'
house at Rye by Mr. Belloc and another,
unshaven and dishevelled but vociferous
and irrepressible, his account of the
birthday dinner to Mr. Belloc at which
there were to be no speeches, and at
which everybody present spoke, and his
story of the aged negro porter in America with a face like a walnut whom,
he says, 'I discouraged from brushing
my hat, and who rebuked me saying,
'Ho, young man, yo's losing ye dignity
before yo times. Yo's got to look nice
for the girls.'

"The sketches of his friends and those
of the many public men with whom he
came in contact are of extraordinary
interest. In a few lines he paints sharp
and unforgettable portraits not only of
his intimate friends but of men and

women with whom he had perhaps but one short conversation. It is thus he tells of his meeting with King George V at the house of the late Lord Burnham. He sums up his impression of 'about as genuine a person as I ever met' in these words—'If it should ever happen that I hear before I die among new generations who never saw George the Fifth that he is being praised either as a strong silent man, or depreciated as a stupid and empty man, I shall know that history has got the whole portrait wrong.'

"There are brilliant little sketches of George Wyndham, Charles Masterman and Cunninghame Graham, among many others; of each one it is the true thing and the generous thing that he sets down. No less arresting are the little cameos of wholly unknown men and women who said or did something that left an impression on his receptive and retentive mind. For example there was the 'huge healthy simple-faced man of the plastering profession' who at a Penny Reading, being unable to endure further recitations about to be provided by a gentleman who had already obliged with 'The Charge of the Light Brigade' and 'The May Queen,' 'arose slowly in the middle of the room like some vast Leviathan arising from the ocean and observed, 'Well, I've just 'as

11

about enough of this. **Good** evening,
Mr. Ash **Good** evening, ladies and gen-
tlemen,' and shouldered his way out of
the Progressive Hall with an unaffected
air of complete amiability and profound
relief.'

"Memorable as are all the records of
his outer life, the insight that he gives
us into his mental and spiritual develop-
ment is of deeper significance. It would
be impossible, for me at least, to sum-
marize the subjective side of this autobiography. To be understood, even to
be partly understood, it must be read
in its entirety. Many readers will not
be able to accept the conclusions to
which Chesterton found himself inevit-
ably driven, but none can fail to see
that his steadfast faith, his sure hope,
and his abounding charity were the out-
come of no slipshod or haphazard
thought, but of mental processes to
which he gave the whole of his clear
and original mind, and that in his life-
long struggle towards the light which
he felt assured he had ultimately found
he was as completely honest with himself as he always was in his dealings
with his fellow men.

"This is a noble record of a noble
life."

## CHAPTER TWO

## LITERARY APPRENTICESHIP

Chesterton had a shorter apprenticeship for a writing career than most men of letters. After leaving St. Paul's he went to the Slade Art School where he graduated in 1891 at the age of seventeen. He forthwith began reviewing books on art for the "Bookman," the "Speaker," and other periodicals. In 1901 he married Frances Blogg whom he had known for some time. Among those present at the wedding was Miss Elizabeth Yeats, the sister of the poet William Butler Yeats, who recalls,

"My sister and I were at the Chesterton's wedding at St. Mary's Abbots in Kensington. Gilbert wanted the ceremony as ceremonial as possible—but Frances, who then belonged to some new thought people in religious matters, wanted everything possible cut from the Church of England Service— except just the legal parts. Gilbert had been, of course, brought up a nonconformist."

Chesterton's marriage was the beginning of thirty-five years of happiness with a wife who was ideally congenial.

13

His first book "Greybeards at Play," consisting of jingles and sketches, had appeared in 1894. As time went on he gradually found the expression of ideas more satisfying than any kind of art work.[†]

From 1898 to 1901 he and his brother Cecil helped Hilaire Belloc on "The New Witness," a weekly paper pledged to wage eternal against political corruption. Some years earlier he had severed his connections with socialism and adopted Belloc's ideas now known as "Distributism," the progress of which was to be ultimately chronicled by the famous "G. K.'s Weekly" founded in 1926.

Stephen Gwynn recalls the first book written for Macmillan.

"It is so long ago that I only dimly remember my first encounter with G. K. C. He was married and they let a flat—Battersea Park—a tiny flat—in 1901. I never knew two people who changed less in nearly forty years.

"On my advice the Macmillans had asked him to do Browning in the 'English Men of Letters,' when he was still not quite arrived. Old Mr. Craik, the Senior Partner, sent for me and I found him in white fury, with Chesterton's proofs corrected in pencil; or rather not corrected; there were still thirteen er-

---

[†] Frances Chesterton died December 12, 1938.

14

rors uncorrected on one page; mostly in quotations from Browning. A selection from a Scotch ballad had been quoted from memory and three of the four lines were wrong. I wrote to Chesterton saying that the firm thought the book was going to "disgrace" them. His reply was like the trumpeting of a crushed elephant. But the book was a huge success as it deserved to be."

J. Lewis May writes about another early book,

"A book that created something of a sensation in its day was the penetrating study of George Bernard Shaw by Chesterton. The mention of Chesterton reminds me that it was Lane who published his 'Orthodoxy' and his 'Napoleon of Notting Hill,' as well as 'Heretics.' Those, I think, were in the days before the royalty system came in, and I fancy Lane bought them outright. It was in regard to the first that I heard that Chesterton brought it in chapter by chapter as he wrote it, and it was written on any miscellaneous scraps of paper that came to his hand. He did not disdain, I have been told, even the paper that sugar is wrapped in, for the purpose of recording his valuable thoughts. Anatole France was accustomed to use the inside of envelopes or the backs of bills for the same object."

William Platt gave Chesterton encouragement at the start,

"We are all aware that one of G. K. C.'s first successes was by a series of articles signed 'The Defendant' each one being headed 'In Defense of . . . .'

"I wrote immediately to the clever young 'Defendant' telling him of the certainty of his future as a writer. He immediately came 'round to see me. Tall, young, handsome, vivacious. At once we fraternized.

"After that our trends in life became rather diverse. We met occasionally, chiefly at public gatherings in London. At rare intervals we exchanged letters. But G. K. C. never forgot my early prediction of his inevitable rise to fame, or the many things we had in common, in his sense of knight-errantry and mine. In any hall the moment he caught sight of me he would greet me with his radiant smile, or, if free, he would at once come over to me."

A newspaperman once asked Chesterton what he considered his first most important book,

" 'Napoleon of Notting Hill' and I almost missed writing it. If I hadn't written it, I would have stopped writing. I was what you Americans call 'broke'—only ten shillings in my pocket. Leaving my worried wife, I went down Fleet Street, got a shave, and then ordered for myself, at the Cheshire Cheese, an enormous luncheon of my favorite dishes and a bottle of wine. It took my all, but I could then go to my publishers fortified. I told them I wanted to write a book and outlined the story of 'Napoleon of Notting Hill.' But I must have twenty pounds, I said, before I begin.

" 'We will send it to you on Monday.'

" 'If you want the book,' I replied, 'you will have to give it to me today as I am disappearing to write it.' They gave it.'

"Later Chesterton said, 'What a fool a man is, when he comes to the last ditch, not to spend the last farthing to satisfy the inner man before he goes out to fight a battle with wits.' "

Just before the War the Irish Lit-er-a-ry Society had a debate at which G. K. C. was the principal speaker: the Chairman being Stephen Gwynn, and among the other speakers was Jimmy Glover at that time conductor of the Drury Lane orchestra, whose father published the collected edition of Tom Moore's melodies. In introducing Chesterton, Stephen Gwynn chipped him on his life of Browning in the "English Men of Letters Series," and on certain mistakes he had made on it, and wondered why he had undertaken a subject, about which he apparently knew so

17

little. Chesterton, with his usual chuckle and wiping the perspiration from his face on to the lapels of his frock coat, retorted that he had had some doubts on the undertaking, but when he had discovered in the series entitled "English Men of Letters," a life written by an Irishman (Stephen Gwynn) on another Irishman (Tom Moore) he had no further qualms in the matter. The back-chat continued for a time, and Mr. Boyle recalls, ended by Chesterton suggesting that he should get on with the subject of the evening and then proceed with the important matter before them, which was the weighing of himself against Jimmy Glover who had had the audacity to state that he was heavier than the famous author. After the meeting George Boyle had a few words with G. K. C. and reminded him that he was in St. Paul's School with him but that he had been in a higher class than himself. With the same good-natured chuckle G. K. C. said this was quite impossible as he had always remained in the very lowest class he could while at that school.

As known from his "Autobiography," Chesterton wrote a great deal for "The Speaker" under J. L. Hammond's editorship. The latter came to know him through L. R. Oldershaw (an old school friend of his who shared rooms with Hammond at that time in the Temple.) Oldershaw wrote for "The Speaker" (mainly fiction reviewing) and he brought Chesterton to see Hammond. As we can imagine he made a deep impression on Hammond, and on the other young men who worked for "The Speaker." The first contribution he made was an article on Ruskin in the form of a review of a life by W. G. Collingwood. This appeared on April 26th, 1900. The first number of "The Speaker" after it had passed into the hands of a group of Liberals to which Hammond belonged, was published at the beginning of October, 1899.

Chesterton wrote much during the Boer War, including some excellent skits on Chamberlain and other topics at the General Election of 1900.

F. W. Hirst has recollections about "The Speaker":

"As regards G. K. Chesterton, I was partly responsible for publishing his early contributions to 'The Speaker' which I helped edit from 1899 (when I first met him) until after the end of the Boer War. My political cooperation with Chesterton (and Belloc) was mainly due to our antipathy to aggressive imperialism which was shared with Mark Twain."

# CHAPTER THREE

## MEETINGS WITH G. K. C.

Miss Alice Henry of Melbourne, Australia, has kindly pointed out to the author that the following is something which has never had any but ephemeral publication in a newspaper, and yet it is surely one of the most striking messages he ever uttered. Chesterton was the one British writer, utterly unknown before, who built up a great reputation during the South African War, and it was gained, not through nationalistic support, but through determined and persistent opposition to the British policy. After the war ended, he ran a column in the "London Daily News." A correspondent had asked him for a definition of his anti-war attitude. This was his reply,

"The unreasonable patriot is one who sees the faults of his fatherland with an eye which is clearer and more merciless than any eye of hatred, the eye of an irrational and irrevocable love."

The reader will recall that in his "Autobiography" Chesterton states that it was in Fleet Street that he first met Sir Philip Gibbs "who carried a curious air of being the right man in the wrong place."

However, in a letter to the author, Sir Philip disagrees with this,

"As regards G. K. C., he was a good friend of mine and has placed me on record in his 'Autobiography' as 'the right man in the wrong place'—though as a matter of fact I claim to have been the right man in the right place—which was Fleet Street, where he and I met many times as writers for the Press. His books belong to my mental library and he will live in English literature as one of our great essayists, and above all as a good poet."

Sir Oliver Lodge recalls:

"G. K. C. at one time lived at the set of flats in Artillery Mansions where I had one of them, and I used to meet him outside sometimes waiting for a cab in the street and had a few words with him. I also met him at the Synthetic Society dinners, and once I impounded a piece of blotting-paper on which he had made a lot of characteristic scribbles (clever sketches of faces) absentmindedly during a discussion at one of these dinners."

Robert Blatchford, the well known editor of "The Clarion" and author of "Merrie England," who was born away

back in 1851, tells of a long controversy he had with Chesterton in the
press some thirty years ago about de-
terminism: "Some years later he wrote
in some paper, I forgot which, and paid
me the finest compliment I ever received. He said,

" 'Very few intellectual minds have
left such a mark on our time: have cut
so deep or remained so clean. His case
for Socialism, so far as it goes, is so
clear and simple that any one would
understand it when it was put properly:
his genius was that he could put it properly. His triumphs were triumphs of
strong style, active pathos, and picturesque metaphor: his very lucidity
was a generous sympathy with simple
minds. For the rest he had triumphed
with being honest and by not being
afraid.'

"Now in paying me that compliment
he complimented himself, for only a
very warm-hearted and generous man
could have treated an opponent with
such gallantry and kindness. But you
cannot publish that tribute without giving the impression that I am fishing
for a cheap advertisement.

"Then as to his books. I liked what
he wrote about Dickens and some of his
poetry, and I recognize his brilliance:
but a good deal of his work I found

22

rather tiresome, and you cannot publish such an opinion.

"We met several times and got on quite pleasantly together."

W. W. Jacobs, the author of "Many Cargoes," recollects,

"I cannot recall my first meeting with Chesterton: it was so very long ago. But I do remember an occasion when he sat next to me at dinner and said that he had rheumatism so badly that he did not know how he would be able to stand up for his speech. A difficulty which he solved by keeping my right shoulder in a strong hand and bearing down upon it. It was a good speech, but it seemed to be the longest I had ever listened to."

"I regret that I never met G. K. C. personally," laments James Hilton, "but I did when quite a small boy send him a poem I had written (a drinking song as a matter of fact), modeled after his own style, and received a charming letter from his wife, I think, saying that he had been much interested and 'believed that after the war there would be a great recrudescence of drinking songs.' This was my first letter from even the wife of a celebrity and I was very proud of it. As a matter of fact, in my entire life I have only written anything you could call fan letters to two authors, Chesterton on this one occasion, and again later to Galsworthy.

"I wish I could give you more interesting reminiscences of Chesterton, whose work I admire very much, but we were of different generations and it happened that we never met, though we had many mutual friends. I think my favorite book of his is 'The Man Who Was Thursday,' which I remember reading during my school days. I am very pleased to hear from you that he expressed admiration for 'Goodbye Mr. Chips.' I did not know of this and it is a source of deep gratification to me."

Christopher Hollis first met G. K. C. in company with one of Belloc's sons:

"The first time that I met Mr. Chesterton was, when as an undergraduate at Oxford, I was in the company of Hilary Belloc, the son of Mr. Belloc, to see the Association Football Cup Final —the culminating event of the English football season—at Wembley. We were traveling by motor bicycle from Oxford to Wembley and, passing through Beaconsfield in the middle of the morning, Hilary Belloc took me to pay a call on Mr. Chesterton, whom we found walking in the garden with his wife."

And Hilaire Belloc himself:

"I met Mr. Chesterton first when I was thirty, and he, I think, twenty-six. That was at the end of the year 1900.

24

I had already written and spoken for some years on what later became known as 'Distributism.' I do not think that he had by that time written or spoken upon public affairs."

Gilbert Frankau is "afraid that I only met G. K. Chesterton once. This was at a debate. He took the chair and was, I remember, a little sarcastic about my own contribution. But the sarcasm was so beautifully done that it became almost a compliment. He really had a rare charm of manner. And he really was a character. Characters being only too rare in this modern world where all tend to become stereotyped. I was, of course, a Father Brown fan. But which really made the deepest impression on my young mind was Chesterton's poetry. It had, for me, the supreme virtue of vigor."

The critic Coulson Kernahan admired Chesterton hugely:

"The first time I met him was when he was lunching with dear old Robert Barr at the Savage Club. Barr came over to my table to say 'Chesterton is my guest and I told him who you were.' He said 'Kernahan and I are two of the rather uncommon authors, today, who write of serious and religious subjects. I'd like to meet him.' 'So come over to my table, Kernahan, and meet him.'

"I did. At about two o'clock Barr had to leave to keep an editorial engagement, and I said to G. K. C. 'I am a member. Won't you stay on as my guest now your host is going?' He did. He stayed till six o'clock, talking brilliantly all the time (with an interlude for tea—'till then he had enjoyed the club's excellent wine), and never once repeated himself. Then we met again at the Centenary Celebration of George MacDonald. Ramsay MacDonald was President of the Centenary Memorial, with Chesterton and myself as Vice-Presidents, and G. K. C. was one of the speakers, and very happy and interesting in what he said.

"My last meeting with him was in Hastings. My wife and I were passing the Queen's Hotel on the front, and I heard myself hailed by name. It was G. K. C. sitting outside in the sun at a table, with a bottle of wine before him, and he invited us to come and share it, and as many more bottles as we felt inclined for. Once again, he talked in that brilliant paradoxical and 'intriguing' way of his and for hours on at a time. My wife and I came away with his musical, but rather high voice, still in our ears, and with new and many beautiful, but sometimes perplexing thoughts, born of what that man of genius had said, in our minds.

"That, alas, is all I can tell you of G. K. C. But if you can get sight of my book 'Celebrities' which I think Dutton published in America, you will find G. K. C. figuring there as Judge, (Bernard Shaw as Foreman and myself as one of the Jury), at the much discussed Edwin Drood trial held in the June before the war by the Dickens Fellowship of which I was, and still am, a Vice-President. Chesterton, as I say in my book, took the part of Judge seriously and finely, for we wished to come to some discovery about Edwin Drood. But Bernard Shaw 'guyed' the show, and turned a serious inquiry into a farce."

Eric Gill, the well known sculptor, recalls,

"Apart from seeing Chesterton many times at meetings I don't think I actually met him in a personal way until about 1925 on the occasion of the founding of 'G. K.'s Weekly,' when I stayed the night at his house and we discussed the policy of his paper, especially with reference to industrialism and art. After we came to live here (which is only a few miles from Beaconsfield) we saw him more often."

A party of members of St. George's Rambling Society, devoted to historical and archaeological research were visiting Beaconsfield on a pleasant afternoon in the September of 1935. They called upon the author at his home, "Top Meadow." Mrs. Chesterton received them with much courtesy, and while they were talking to her, he came into the Lounge Hall of his house, which was fitted up in the Tudor style, with large fireplace, around which everyone grouped. They rose when he entered, and he soon engaged all in conversation. He was in excellent form. His first question, "What really did you come here to see?" was promptly answered by one of the members, Fred H. Postans, "We came to see Mr. Chesterton." He then told an amusing anecdote against himself. He had been much annoyed by the noise made by the local film studios quite close to his home, and after sending several ineffectual letters of protest, eventually asked his secretary to call upon the manager of the studios. Upon doing so, that lady made a strong protest saying emphatically, "The position is becoming impossible . . . . Mr. Chesterton can't write," to which the manager replied, "We were well aware of that." He relished the telling of this story immensely. He went on to give some local details about Beaconsfield. It was asked him whether he ever intended to write a Life of Dr. Samuel Johnson, and he said he thought that had al-

ready been done very well by Boswell.
Postans pointed out that there was a
little too much Boswell in that, in his
opinion. He seemed to agree and said
that he greatly admired the Doctor and
it was not entirely impossible that he
might undertake to write his life.

"My only meeting with Chesterton,"
writes Hugh Kingsmill, "was in the autumn of 1912, when I went to Beaconsfield to interview him for 'Hearth and
Home,' which was being edited by
Frank Harris. One of his arms was in a
sling, and he found great difficulty in
pouring out drink. To my surprise he
was not quaffing ale but sipping a
liqueur. He insisted however in pouring the drinks for both of us, out of
courtesy. He seemed to me very absent-minded and gentle, and I formed an
extremely pleasant impression of him.
At the same time he did not strike me
as at all alive to ordinary existence.
His praise of the man in the street and
of common life has always seemed to me
a defense thrown up against his own
temperament. I think he was naturally
an artist and poet of the self-absorbed,
rather limited kind, and that he was
afraid of this tendency, and fled to
democracy, Dickens and eventually the
Roman Church, in order not to lapse
into pure aestheticism. As far as I
know, and I have met many of them,

29

his friends were drawn from rather cranky people, not from normal types, and this illustrates the division between his opinions and his temperament. He was not a good judge of individuals, in my opinion. Nothing could be further from the truth than his picture of Dickens as a roistering lover of the poor. On the other hand, his intelligence was very acute in the destructive criticism of the fads and poses against which he was always contending. If he did not understand ordinary life, he certainly understood the aesthetes, faddists and millenarians of the twenty years before the war, and made brilliant game of them in 'Heretics.' Since the war, his work seems to me to have fallen off greatly. I have seen him several times, wandering about the streets or in Marylebone station, and was touched by his melancholy look. I think life depressed him. In his youth he praised the poor man's literature of thrillers and shockers. In his later life he denounced the cinema. What the distinction, at any rate in mind, between printed nonsense and visible nonsense is, he never explained. I attribute this change of fact that as he grew older, he could not summon up enough energy to continue his celebration of the man in the street, and was more concerned with finding seasons for his faith in his last refuge from a perplexing world, the Roman Catholic Church.

"But he did a valuable work in destructive criticism, and he was a lovable figure. I cannot think of any other well-known writer of the day in England whom one would not sooner spare from the scene than G. K. My friend Hesketh Pearson was staying with me when I read of Chesterton's death. I told him of it through the bathroom door, and he sent up a hollow groan which must have been echoed that morning all over England."

Philip Guedalla recollects, "I first saw Gilbert Chesterton on the occasion of a visit of his to Oxford when I was an undergraduate 'round about 1909 or 1910. It was a dark vision of the inside of a four-wheeled cab almost entirely filled with Chesterton. From its interior an arm and hand emerged and proceeded to struggle wildly with the outside handle of the vehicle. There was a College debate the same evening of which Chesterton was the opener; and I was offered up to him as the only undergraduate with insufficient impudence to attempt this suicidal controversy. He came back with me to my room in College and performed two acts which would have struck him as sacramentally Chestertonian. First he sat through my only arm chair to its destruction; then he finished all my whisky. On the next morning I piously presented for signature by its author a copy of 'Orthodoxy' and was profoundly shocked when he inscribed it 'BOSH BY G. K. CHESTERTON.'"

"Yes, I should be delighted to go on record as one of the admirers of G. K. Chesterton," writes Clements Ripley. "He has always been an enthusiasm of mine. The first book of his I ever read was 'The Man Who Was Thursday.' I couldn't have been more than fourteen when I picked this up and of course a great deal of the symbolism and the metaphysical quality of the book escaped me at that age. I read it for the story and it was a very fast moving and fascinating story. I think even then I appreciated the brilliancy of Chesterton's paradoxical style, although at that time I certainly wouldn't have called it that."

"It seems hardly possible," ponders Walter de la Mare, "that a human being with the least claim to a vestige of intelligence should have forgotten his first meeting with G. K. C. I am, however, that unfortunate kind of man, and cannot even remember my first observations on entering this (at least) exceptionally interesting world.' I recall most vividly, of course, many meetings and these memories are not in the slightest degree composite ones—even if memories ever are composite. And so vividly, indeed, that it all but amounts to an hallucination—as if we were meeting again!

"Like how many, many friends of his, I have the greatest affection for, and admiration of, his work—and how much his work was he himself, though not, of course, all himself! That, I suppose, can never be."

"There is in London a distinguished Society," declares Marie Belloc Lowndes, "called The Wiseman Dining Society. As its name implies. it is a Catholic Society, but no distinction is made with regard to the religion of the speakers. A great number of outstanding men and women have delivered addresses on every kind of subject of interest to an educated man and woman. The net thrown has been large, among those who have spoken being people as different as Lord Cecil (of the League of Nations), Algernon Blackwood, the famous novelist, Liddell Hart, the most noted military critic in the English-speaking world, and Bernard Pares, the great authority on Russia. Of them all, and the Society has been in existence now for something like ten years— by far the most interesting, and the most beautifully delivered address, was that of G. K. C. on Joan of Arc. This

33

was the more remarkable, as to the best of my belief, Chesterton was not celebrated in this country as a speaker. I myself never heard him speak in public, but on that one occasion. No reporters can be admitted to these dinners because a very free discussion follows every paper read, so I fear no record of the speech exists."

Father Owen F. Dudley records, "I remember still quite vividly my first meeting with Mr. Chesterton and having tea with him in his house in Beaconsfield, Bucks. He was tremendously jovial over H. G. Wells, whom we discussed, and whom he considered a thinker who always stopped thinking. As I watched him, I realized that all the jokes that were bubling out of him, as well as the epigrams, would in all probability appear in some article or book. Mrs. Chesterton and the Secretary were at tea and it struck me as one of the cheeriest households I had ever been in."

# CHAPTER FOUR

---

## SOME FRIENDS

"There's nothing worth the wear of living
   Save laughter and the love of friends."

No one believed more in these words of his friend Hilaire Belloc than Chesterton himself. He delighted in thousands of steadfast friends and acquaintances, and they rejoiced in his inimitable wisdom and good fellowship.

The novelist, Isabel C. Clark, first met him in 1929 when he and his wife lunched with her at Piazza Grazioli: "I cannot remember that he said anything at all amusing or arresting, resembling in this the late Lytton Strachey and Kenneth Graham so that I imagine few authors are as loquacious as myself. But then I am not a man of genius!

"When I saw him he was fifty-five years of age but looked at least ten years more, probably on account of his enormous bulk about which he was fond of joking; indeed I believe he was proud of resembling Dr. Johnson in this respect.

"I heard him lecture on Henry VIII here at the Convent of the Holy Child when he said that Henry had no intention of Protestantizing the Church in England but thought he could have a Catholic Church with himself at the head of it, and that he was astonished to discover how rapidly it disintegrated into many sects. I remember his saying on this occasion: 'Many people are prejudiced against Henry VIII because he was a Large Fat Man,' and then going off into a chuckle of laughter, swelling himself out to an enormous size as he spoke. His wife told me he always rather spoilt his own jokes by laughing at them before he uttered them."

Ralph Adams Cram met him first in London a good many years ago: "Father Wagget asked my wife and myself once when we were staying in London, whom we would like best to meet—'anyone from the King downward.' We chose Chesterton who was a very particular friend of Father Wagget. At that time we put on a dinner at the Buckingham Palace Hotel (in those days the haunt of all the County families) and in defiance of fate, had this dinner in the public dining room. We had as guests

36

Father Wagget, G. K. C. and Mrs. Chesterton. The entrance into the dining room of the short processional created something of a sensation amongst the aforesaid County families there assembled. Father Wagget, thin, cropheaded monk in cassock and rope; G. K. C., vast and practically globular; little Mrs. Chesterton, very South Kensington in moss green velvet; my wife, and myself.

"The dinner was a riot. I have the clearest recollection of G. K. C. seated ponderously at the table, drinking champagne by magnums, continually feeding his face with food which, as he was constantly employed in the most dazzling and epigrammatic conversation, was apt to fall from his fork and rebound from his corporosity, until the fragments disappeared under the table.

"He and Father Wagget egged each other on to the most preposterous amusements. Each would write a triolet for the other to illustrate. They were both as clever with the pencil as with the pen, and they covered the backs of menus with most astonishing literary and artistic productions. I particularly remember G. K. C. suddenly looking out of the dining room window towards Buckingham Palace and announcing that he was now prepared 'to write a disloyal triolet.' This was during the reign of King Edward VII, and the result was convincing. I have somewhere the whole collection of these literary productions with their illustrations, but where they are, I do not know."

"Ten or fifteen years ago," recollects Stephen Gwynn, whom we have already quoted, "Barrie had taken a big house for August, and there was a large party, including several schoolboys and the Chestertons. It was decided to play the game of clues, and in the evening a dozen or more of us were each given bits of paper containing some mystification in verse. At the end all the clues led us to a most amusing charcoal portrait of Lord Beaverbrook. Everybody went to bed, and I was settling down to a quite chat with G. K. C. over whiskey and soda when three schoolboys filed past. 'Thank you very much,' they said to him, 'for giving us an amusing evening.'

"Next morning I said to the spokesman's mother, 'Your youngster said his piece very well.' But she knew nothing about it. It had been the schoolboy's own idea. Admittedly the Chestertons were the best guests in that gathering of a long and very mixed list.

"I remember how Lord David Cecil when still a boy, sitting up there one night and expounding to us two elders the point of view of the younger generation. Not only the easiest man in the world to talk with, but also a very good listener."

Lucille Borden, the novelist, found G. K.'s personality was even more impressive than the things he put to paper: "I remember once on meeting him I asked him what he thought of a certain small English boy (who calls us Aunt-Uncle though we are no relation) who used to plot out London in sections, selecting the men of prominence in those sections, then call on them. This between the ages of nine and thirteen. He was very small and fragile, and by reason of this, all flunkies and secretaries let him pass. So he not only gained access to the great man but used to go and sit with him, looking for all the world like Tiny Tim.

" 'Indeed I remember that boy—he was an extraordinary chap. He will go far but he needs a guiding hand.' . . . This after the boy had grown. The thing that was so remarkable was, that Terence had only his inquisitive personality to recommend him. He has gone far but without the guiding hand, and drifted into the set pseudo-literati, sponsored by the Sitwells. However, at the age of eighteen or nineteen he married—a very clever young woman over whom the London newspapers fought and whom the "Daily Mail" finally acquired—as one of their top-notch women. This gives Terry leisure to write terrible but correct poetry—and to carry on a most extraordinary and original literary career.

"Back to 'nos moutons'—we've seen Gilbert Chesterton start a broadcast-speech to a club on whose Board I am —for which he was allowed forty minutes: He rose from the speakers' table —put his watch in front of him—began one of the most stirring prose poems to which we all ever listened—made his introduction—points in phases as colorful as a rainbow—approached his conclusion — made his logical deductions and finished on the fortieth minute. It was such a tour de force as was rarely done in the earliest days of radio."

"When I was introduced to Chesterton," writes Adolphe de Castro, "I was a bit abashed. He was so formidable and such a mighty eater. But his conversation and his wit were delightful. I have my doubts if any one ever had the temerity to ask Mr. Chesterton why he had embraced Catholicism. I asked him. Americans in those days were forgiven much, and a friend of the late Ambrose Bierce was a particularly privileged character. Chesterton twirled the end of his scraggly moustache for some time, then he said: 'Because of its primitivity.'

" 'Then you ought to have become a Jew,' I said. 'Judaism has greater primitivity.'

"To which he rejoined: 'It has too much primitivity and is not sufficiently elastic for adaptability.'

" 'You hold with Heine that Judaism is not a religion but a misfortune?' I asked.

" 'Heine was a great poet,' returned Chesterton. 'And do you recall what John Locke said, 'A merchant lies for gain; a poet lies for pleasure.' 'Do you happen to write poetry?'

"I put my hand in my pocket and pulled out a sheaf of papers, extracted one and gave it to him. He read it. 'I like this,' he said.

"It was a quasi sonnet entitled 'The Jewish Poet.'

"At one time I doubted the existence of G. K. C.," declares Holbrook Jackson. "I listened to the stories of him as one listens to the yarns of men who have been in the ends of the earth. And even now, after I have looked upon him with my own eyes, I have to nudge myself to realize his probability. He has the reality of one of those dragons or fairies in which he has such invincible faith. I first beheld him on a Yorkshire moor far from his natural ele-

41

ment, which is in London. He was in
the locality on a holiday, and I had gone
over to verify his existence just as one
might go to the Arctic regions to verify
the existence of the North Pole or the
Northwest Passage.

"He was staying at the house of a
Bradford merchant adjoining the moor,
and I was to meet him there. It was
April and raining. I trudged through
the damp furze and heather up to the
house only to find that the object of
my pilgrimage had disappeared without
leaving a trace behind him. No alarm
was felt, as that was one of his habits.
Sometimes he would go down to the
railway station, and taking a ticket to
any place that had a name which appealed to him, vanish into the unknown,
making his way home on foot or wheel
as fancy or circumstances directed. On
this occasion, however, nothing so serious had happened. Therefore I ad-
journed with the lady of the house and
Mrs. Chesterton to an upper hall, where
a noble latticed wnidow commanded a
wide vista of the moor. I peered into
the wild, half hoping that I should first
behold the great form of Gilbert Chesterton looming over the bare brow of
the wold, silhouetted against the grey
sky like the symbol of a large new faith.

"His coming was not melodramatic;
it was, on the contrary, quite simple,

42

quite idyllic, and quite characteristic. In fact, he did not come at all, rather was it that our eyes, and later our herald, went to him. For quite close to the house we espied him, hatless and negligently clad in a Norfolk suit of homespun, leaning in the rain against a budding tree, absorbed in the pages of a little red book.

"This was a most fitting vision. It suited admirably his unaffected, careless, and altogether childlike genius. He came into the house shortly afterwards and consumed tea and cake like any mortal and talked the talk of Olympus with the abandonment and irresistibility of a child. I found his largeness wonderfully proportionate, even, as is so rarely the case with massive men, to his head. This is amply in keeping with the rest of his person. He wears a tangled mass of light brown hair prematurely streaked with grey, and a slight moustache. His grey-blue eyes laugh happily as his full lips unload themselves of a constant flow of self-amused and piquant words. Like Dr. Johnson whom he resembles so much in form, he is a great talker. But while I looked at him I was not reminded of the lexicographer, but of Balzac. And as his monologue rolled on and we laughed and wondered, I found myself carried away to a studio in France, where the head of Chesterton became one with the head of Rodin's conception of France's greatest literary genius.

"Since my first meeting I have seen G. K. C. many times. I have seen him standing upon platforms defending the people's pleasures against the inroads of Puritanism. I have seen him addressing men from a pulpit, and on one memorable occasion at Clifford's Inn Hall I saw him defending the probability of the liquefication of the blood of St. Januarius in the teeth of a pyrotechnic heckling from Bernard Shaw. Again I have seen his vast person dominating the staring throng in Fleet Street like a superman; and I have seen the traffic of Ludgate Circus held up for him, as he strolled by in cloak and combrero like a brigand of Adelphi drama or a Spanish hidalgo by Velasquez, oblivious alike of critical busdriver and wonder-struck multitude.

"But best it is to see him in his favorite habïtat of Bohemian Soho. There in certain obscure yet excellent French restaurants with Hilaire Belloc and other writers and talkers, he may be seen, sitting behind a tall tankard of lager or a flagon of Chiañti, eternally unravelling the mysterious tangle of living ideas; now rising mountainously on his feet to overshadow the company with weighty argument, anon brandish-

ing a wine bottle as he insists upon defending some controversial point until
'we break the furniture'; and always
chuckling at his own wit and the sallies
of others, as he fights the battle of
ideas with indefatigable and unconquer-
able good-humour."

# CHAPTER FIVE

## ON THE ENGLISH PLATFORM

In the course of his life, Chesterton accomplished much lecturing and public speaking as did most of the English writers of his generation such as Shaw, Wells, and to a lesser extent Galsworthy and Bennett. Like many Englishmen his success as a speaker was variable and subject to his health and feelings even more than most men. Yet no matter how indifferently Chesterton might have done in the formal part of his address, he always more than redeemed himself in the question-and-answer period that followed. The speed with which he would answer questions was simply incredible. As one listened to him answering one question after another usually of so unrelated a nature, one marvelled at ability and nimbleness so extraordinary.

The distinguished author R. Ellis Roberts, heard a lecture at Oxford:

"I do not, alas! remember what Mr. Chesterton lectured to us about. I remember the manner of his lecture. It seemed to be written on a hundred written pieces of variously shaped paper, written in ink and pencils (of all colors and in chalk). All the papers were in a splendid and startling disorder, and I remember being at first just a little disappointed. Then the papers were abandoned, and G. K. C. talked, and we got more and more interested and pleased. I remember a passage about cathedrals and railway stations which aroused opposition; and with opposition and question the real Chesterton broke loose. He will, I am sure, if he reads this in the next world, forgive me for saying that to myself I whispered 'Elephant'. All day the image had been present with me of something vast and weighty, incredibly simple, incalculably wise, and unquestionably kindly. Foolishly I mourned a certain sluggishness. Then as I say, came opposition; and suddenly—trunk up, roaring, speeding, faster and faster—the wisest of us was pursuing his trifling opponents through quickset hedge and over ploughed fields of argument. How he raced! I know, because of all the opposition none ran faster than I!"

"My own acquaintance with Chesterton," Father Francis J. Yealy, S. J., writes "has been gained from his books and from one of his lectures delivered in Cambridge, England, in 1925. Just outside the town of Cambridge is a vil-

lage called Chesterton, the Anglican
vicar of which sat on the stage during
the lecture. Afterwards he made a short
speech, inviting G. K. to visit the vil-
lage and, I believe, suggesting that it
might have been named after his an-
cestors. At any rate Chesterton responded gracefully and played most
amusingly with this identity of names.
It was possible, he said, that the place
had been named after one of his an-
cestors, but it seemed more likely that
the family had taken their name from
it. Perhaps they had lived there in the
remote past under a different name,
and one of them, who would no doubt
have been a worthless fellow, had eventually been run out of town. The natural
place to go was of course Cambridge;
and the people there with their great
kindliness allowed him to loiter about.
In time he became a familiar figure in
Cambridge; but, as no one knew his
name, they began to refer to him as the
fellow from Chesterton and later simply
as Chesterton. This he thought was
very reasonable theory of the origin of
his name." .

"One day in February, 1902," records
Mr. Karl H. Harklander, "I happened
to notice on the announcing board of
the Leeds University that a G. K. Chesterton would lecture about 'Man, Great
Man, Super-man.' I was a young tex-

tile manufacturer on a business journey and hungered for more than 'bread alone!' That night I heard the best and also the shortest lecture of my life; in less than twenty minutes our assembly was quite clear about 'Man, Great man, Super-man.' I marked my young 'man' who might become super-man,' but who chose to be 'great man' in accordance with the exposition of the 1902 lecture."

A charming reminiscence comes from Edward Brown:

"In 1927 the great man accepted the Honorary Presidency of the University College of Wales (Aberystwyth) Debates Union. The undergraduates resolved that he should be conveyed from the station to the Queen's Hotel in a manner worthy of his greatness and of our reputation for hospitality. An old fashioned vehicle of the 'growler' variety was dug out from the lumber yard of an inn and some of the dust and signs of neglect were removed therefrom.

"As Secretary of Debate's Union I demanded and won, the privilege of driving this state coach. Our Officers Training Corps received permission to act as escort but were refused the privilege of carrying arms. They accordingly armed themselves with hoes, rakes, spades, axes, etcetera.

49

"It had been arranged that the President of the Union should sit with Chesterton ('back to the engine') and the President of Ladies' Hostel . . . . . fortunately a very small lady . . . . with Mrs. Chesterton. But as soon as the two guests had taken their seats, the O. T. C. rushed the coach and some half dozen of them secured a seat or footing of some sort. A burly sergeant with battle axe (borrowed from the Art Department) sat beside Mrs. Chesterton facing G. K. C. My stolid steeds were replaced by forty undergraduates, and we tore through the narrow streets at a most reckless pace."

In reply to the demand for a speech, G. K. C. stood at the top of Queen's Hotel steps and said,

"You need never be ashamed of the athletic prowess of this College. The Pyramids, we are told, were built by slave labor. But the slaves were not expected to haul the pyramids in one piece!"

In his address that evening he commented on the ancient custom of sending a condemned man to his death in the same coach as the executioner; and described his feelings as he faced the great axe in the coach. Later he presented the "executioner" with an exquisite caricature of them both with the

50

axe between them. The caricature now hangs in the Men's Union.

An Honorary President of the Debate Union at Aberystwyth is always elected by the D. U. Committee (all students, save for one Lecturer). The name is submitted to the Senate for its approval. The Debate Union was formed from an amalgamation of the Literary and Debating Society and the Political Union in 1925 about a year before G. K. C.'s Presidency. Chesterton was succeeded by John Drinkwater, John van Druten, and Sir Arthur Quiller-Couch.

G. K. C.'s speech was on "Liberty: the Last Phrase," by which he explained he meant the latest phase. Just as barons had fought against the tyranny of would-be despots, just as yeoman had fought those same barons for freedom of property and action, just as . . . etc. factory-hands; electors . . . so ought men today to band in a great crusade to defend the common man's freedom of the highway, a freedom which was being denied him by the motorist. The cause was obscured by the common man's desire to join the enemy as soon as his means permitted him to do so. Envy of our enemy inspired a desire to emulate him. His chariots were objects of admiration, instead of loathing and furious hostility

. . . But the fact remained that our roads, our ancient highways were being wrested from us. "The price of liberty is eternal vigilance."

The Senior History Lecturer and some others were of the opinion that the whole thesis of the address was a gigantic leg-pull!

The students that evening were a songful crowd, and they had evolved in G. K. C.'s honour a parody of a well-known Salvation Army hymn that went, "I'm H-A-P-P-PY, I know I am, I'm sure I am, I'm H-A-P-P-Y!"

They had already several parodies on that spelling motif, such as "I'm D-R-U-N-K!"

That evening as G. K. C. entered, they all burst into, "I'm G. K. Chester—TON," with terrific and increasing emphasis on the TON, later varying it "G. K. . . . . Just-a TON." The great man was delighted and bowed, smiled, and clapped his hands.

Of Chesterton in Liverpool Mr. Clarence Fry recalls, "I was living in Liverpool at the time Mr. Chesterton joined the Roman Catholic Church. Having been charmed with his writings, I went to see and hear him lecture. I remember how disappointed I was with his address (perhaps owing to Protestant prejudices). But I had reckoned without my host. The Chairman said all questions asked on paper would be answered by the Speaker. And then Mr. Chesterton rose and reading out each question, replied in a few pregnant words; immediately sitting down and beaming most angelically all round the hall on the audience, as much as to say, 'How's that! Beat that, if you can!' And in **no** one case could any answer be ventured. I was delighted and overwhelmed with the sense of his masterly dealing with the issues laid before him. The replies were electric in their concise power. Also, as you may believe, I was charmed with his whole personality."

The chairman was the late Roman Catholic Archbishop of Liverpool, Dr. Keating, supported by the Catholic Bishop of Birmingham and other dignitaries. The occasion aroused great interest, as not long before G. K. C. had joined the Catholic Church. The meeting was arranged so that this new "Defender of the Faith" might help **the** cause of Catholicism in the city. The speech was largely devoted to an exposition of his newly-found faith.

"Chesterton seldom came to Glasgow," records George Mortimer, "and the only time I heard him was on his first visit to the city one Sunday evening fully thirty years ago when he lectured in the Berkeley Hall which seats about six hundred people. His subject was 'Some New Dangers of Oligarchies.' In those days Sunday evening lectures were not popular in Scotland, and neither are they now. The churches are in most cases meagrely attended in the evening, the majority of people either going for a walk, visiting their friends or remaining at home and listening to the wireless.

"Evidently G. K. Chesterton, whom I had first seen referred to years previously as a new Carlyle, proved a powerful magnet, for instead of going to church I traveled from Paisley to Glasgow—seven miles by tramcar. All I remember about the meeting is that the hall was well filled; that a Scottish author, David Lowe, at present contributing reminiscences which he calls 'Lowe Life' to a Glasgow paper, was chairman; that Chesterton, then thirty years of age, was a large and fleshy man with a fine head of luxuriant brown hair; and that he made reference to the Boer War, to Lord Rosebery, and to Mr. Parks, a prominent lawyer, business man, Methodist and Liberal M. P., I have a general impression that he showed himself a democrat."

"Chesterton was a past master of the art known popularly as 'pulling your leg,'" according to Mr. William Platt. "With him, this was not merely a man-

54

ifestation of his exuberant temperament; it was also a matter of principle, a determination to make the other man see that there are two sides to every question.

"I remember well his address to the British Humanitarian League. This body was of excellent principles, and supported by many and able and eminent persons; but it also contained many who had become rabid and fanatical, and so provided targets, for G. K. C.

" 'If' he said 'you ask me to extend my sympathy to the poor fox, pursued by savage sportsmen, shall I not also extend it to the poor sportsman, pursued by savage humanitarians?'

"And he proceeded to draw a contrast between the typical elderly colonel, who ought by profession to be a man of blood, but who in point of fact was the kindest and mildest of men, and the typical humanitarian, who ought to be brimming over with human kindness, but who on the contrary was furiously ready to assail any unfortunate who happened in his or her opinion to transgress the code.

"Bernard Shaw was present, and during the debate received a delicious setback from a witty Irishman called Connel. 'Shaw is out to persuade us to be vegetarians,' he said; 'but if we all adopt that creed, what would happen?

55

Rabbits would obey the Scriptural command to increase and multiply until they overran the whole country-side and ate up every vegetable; and where then would Mr. Bernard Shaw get his daily bunch of carrots?'

"Despite Chesterton's ability to state the other side, and to state it wittily and well, he was no mere arguer for argument's sake. He would not put forward any viewpoint unless he was convinced that there was ground for his support. He hated that type of politician or publicist who from sheer intellectual dexterity could argue in favor of any cause that it paid him to support, probably with his tongue in his cheek. This is very clearly seen in his brilliant retort to Lord Birkenhead, ending with that overwhelming:— 'Chuck it, Smith!'

"Probably the finest instance of the effective use of slang by a great literary stylist!

"When he spoke to me about my work he used to say:—

" 'What I admire about your idealism, as shown in your writings, is the fact that I know it to be genuine. For writers who merely pay lip-service to ideals, because they think it safest to do so, I have no use whatever. But I know that what you say, you mean.'

"Chesterton, like most artistic persons, had a dislike for officialdom and bureaucracy. It seems so often to lead to a dull and spurious uniformity and standardization. The natural love of the artist is for variety, reaching out to a fullness of life and experience."

"I remember hearing G. K. C. make a very amusing point at a meeting of educationists where he was the chief speaker. He pictured a state of things where the official director of education might be a man with chronic catarrh. Far from realizing this as a deficiency, the official, he supposed, would attempt to impose it on others; to require that all pupils should be told to pronounce English as the director pronounced it. Or, as Chesterton amusingly put it:—

" 'He wadted theb do brodoudce Idglish as he hibself brodoudced it, this bad with the groddig gattarrh. Ibadgidge it for yourselves.'

"To those who never heard G. K. C. speak in public I would say that he stood on the platform as the very essence of good humour. He beamed on all and sundry. He radiated kindliness. He smiled, he laughed, he bubbled over. He was out to enjoy himself and to make every one present enjoy himself. A personification of mirth, good temper and happy humanity."

Prof. A. J. Armstrong, head of the English Department of Baylor Univer-

sity, Waco, Texas, heard G. K. C. in
England,

"He talked to the members of my
group for more than an hour on Browning. He referred to his own life of
Browning as an immature work, although he said it was necessary for him
to do a great deal of hack work when
he was young, about the time of this
publication.

"When one of the ladies present in-
terrupted and said,

" 'Mr. Chesterton, the Browning work
has some wonderful things in it,' he
only laughed and went on. In his
thoughts he stayed close to the things
that he had said in his book. His general conversation, of course, was delightful and was filled with the paradoxes for which he was so famous."

"He took dinner with us at the Hotel
Victoria, off Trafalgar Square, and Mrs.
Chesterton was with him. I sat next
Mrs. Chesterton the whole evening and
she was a lovely woman, quiet, refined,
a poetess, with a great many experiences which she told delightfully.

"Mr. Chesterton had a delightful wit,
was a vigorous speaker, and was a man
of great power,—although—and I believe that this is not given with what
one usually knows of him—he had a
shy way of looking under his glasses
that was charming.

"A little later we had our symposium
58

in London where Mr. Chesterton addressed a group of friends. I do not know whether you ever heard of Mrs. French - Sheldon or not. Before her death all the "Who's Who" carried her. She was an American who learned her 'A B C's' from Washington Irving, and from that time until her death her life was one long spectacle. She told me that at one time she was the guest of George Sand, and that Chopin came in, and Victor Hugo later joined them. Just imagine such a coterie!

"Mrs. French-Sheldon was one who did a great deal of exploring in Africa, and was the first white woman to enter one side of the African Continent and come out on the other. Later under the direction of J. B. Pond, she made twenty-three addresses in America and received $23,000 in cash for them, that is, one thousand dollars a night."

"When I was interested in getting Mr. Chesterton to speak in Waco his fee was one thousand dollars. So in London when I introduced Mrs. French-Sheldon in the charming coterie, I said to Mr. Chesterton: 'Probably when you were a little boy in short trousers this lady was touring American cities at one thousand dollars a night, so you can see that you are not the only one that gets that price, and she got it twenty years before you did.' Mr. Chesterton

59

answered with a smile. But he seemed tremendously impressed, for in the social hour that followed the symposium, he shcwed Mrs. French-Sheldon a number of courtesies."

Mrs. Lillian Curt heard a lecture in London,

"His large body was rather picturesque, but one received a shock when a tiny, high pitched voice emanated from it. I ·vell remember on one occasion before the War that G. K. C. was asked to speak in the large Town Hall of Battersea. The occasion was the Annual Soiree of the West Lambeth Association of Teachers—a large and important local gathering of learned folk and their friends. G. K. C. then in his prime, was the lion of the evening and the lion was expected to roar when his turn came. But no, G. K. C. stood, like a huge cherub, emitting little squeaky phrases. The teachers huddled closer together and craned their necks forward. G. K. C. went on unconcernedly and those who could hear, heard gems of the first (literally) water pour from those curved lips. Not that one sentence had much to do with the last, but each was a superb thought complete in itself and miraculously moulded. I was there, so I know—and enjoyed a delightful tete-a-tete with him and his charming wife afterwards. He was in strange

60

contrast with his brother Cecil—a little man, wee-proportioned, with a charming literary style and good lecture-voice, who fell in the Great European war."

In 1928 Chesterton spoke before the Summer Course at the Victoria and Albert Museum. Mr. Charles A. Eva recalls that it was a sweltering hot July day, and when Chesterton turned up late owing to a train delay, he began his discourse by remarking,

"This is no sort of weather for lecturing or listening, as the lecturer on this occasion can rely on the weather, and not on himself, to send the audience to sleep."

# CHAPTER SIX

## ON THE AMERICAN PLATFORM

Chesterton made two extended visits to the United States, in 1920-1, and in 1930-1. Both times he traversed the length and breadth of the country, delivering innumerable lectures, making many addresses, and participating in not a few debates. No matter what the occasion he never forget his sense of humor. At the Soldiers' Memorial Hall, Pittsburgh, he was introduced to a large audience by Bishop Hugh C. Boyle. When G. K. stood up there arose a collective audible gasp at the enormous size of the man making his way to the amplifier. His opening words were,

"At the outset I want to reassure you I am not this size, really; dear no, I'm being amplified by the thing."

He debated with Cosmo Hamilton at the Brooklyn Academy of Music on November 26th, 1930. The subject of debate was presumably unknown to the two authors, and was announced by the Chairman William C. Redfield, Secretary of Commerce under Wilson, "Is Immorality in the Novel Justified."

The audience was composed chiefly of educators, priests, college instructors, and grade teachers; all seemed properly pleased by the title of the evening's discourse, and settled back to enjoy the action . . . . Chesterton annihilating his gracious and graceful opponent. They were not denied. Chesterton scored decidedly when he showed that what is moral is justified, and that the contrary, of course, could never be justified.

This Chesterton explained in his introductory remarks, which he took from written notes, as Hamilton also did when he arose. Apparently they were formulated, and used in more than one debate in their tour. Chesterton charmingly denied he was there to make a football of Hamilton, who had protested such, but that he was rather a football in appearance, even if on the side of the angels, and Hamilton more the lithe athlete. After these amenities, Chesterton divided his argument into three sections: immorality in the novel violates . . . . first, good morals; second, good manners; third, good taste.

"You can't discuss inflaming the passions without doing it," Chesterton pointed cut. In reply to a query from Hamilton, "On the contrary, I like and admire very much the works of Aldous Huxley, but, (here he showed genuine

63

anger) as for that weak, sniveling, dirty, pacifistic Enrique Maria Remarque, I have nothing but contempt."

Chesterton made many notes, chuckling to himself as he scribbled something soon to come forth as a sally, pausing now and then to survey the audience or his opponent, and again interrupting his writing to place his pencil between his teeth to applaud some remark of Hamilton's.

"Chesterton's voice was a fairly high tenor," recalls Mr. Daniel Kern who was present, "not at all surprising. I have observed that many Englishmen despite bulk and great size, possess the same type voice. For example, H. G. Wells' . . . . so high and snuffled that it was execrable coming over the radio. The loud-speaker system made it easy to hear both men. Both speakers were making use of a word which sounded like 'eppitet' or 'epithet,' which in the context could have had no meaning. The people about us were confused. As we became used to their voices, it developed that the word was 'appetite.' You can estimate the frequency of the occurrence of this word in an ethical discussion when it is coupled with the modifiers 'innate' and 'acquired'."

G. K. C.'s pink face, framed by a white mane of hair, isolated by a rumpled dinner jacket, shining beautifully at the audience, caused Kern's companion, a singular personality, to remark wistfully, "Chesterton's just a saint, just a saint."

The warm, human, simple childlike nature, and the beaming benevolence of Chesterton's smile was so utterly charming that Mr. W. D. Hennessy also present, was immediately reminded of two quite disparate characters his "favorite uncle, now deceased and Santa Claus. As I thought more about it, I realized that my first instinctive impression in its childlike simplicity, was founded upon a correct perception. My uncle was loved by every man, woman, child, and dog in his town and he was the most natural democrat I ever knew. I am just as certain that Chesterton was a beloved figure to his neighbors and that he was a true democrat in the best sense of that much abused term.

"Mr. Hamilton several times referred to Chesterton as a cherub and a teacher. G. K. C. expressed difficulty in reconciling the picture of a cherub and a teacher, but I think Cosmo Hamilton's appellations were apt, for was not Chesterton an angelic teacher? And when a casual remark about the New York subway was made by Hamilton, I was delighted at the way G. K. C. pounced upon it as a perfect allegory, comparing

65

the modern world looking for its way with the stranger lost in the labyrinths of the subway."

Mr. Joseph J. Reilly attended a debate at Mecca Temple in New York City, between Chesterton and Clarence Darrow, which dealt with the story of creation as presented in Genesis. It was a Sunday afternoon and the Temple was packed. At the conclusion of the debate everybody was asked to express his opinion as to the victor and slips of paper were passed around for that purpose. The award went directly to Chesterton. Darrow in comparison, seemed heavy, uninspired, slow of mind, while G. K. C. was joyous, sparkling and witty . . . . quite the Chesterton one had come to expect from his books. The affair was like a race between a lumbering sailing vessel and a modern steamer.

Mrs. Frances Taylor Patterson also heard the Chesterton-Darrow debate, but went to the meeting with some misgivings because she was a trifle afraid that Chesterton's "gifts might seem somewhat literary in comparison with the trained scientific mind and rapier tongue of the famous trial lawyer. Instead, the trained scientific mind, the clear thinking, the lightning quickness in getting a point and hurling back an answer, turned out to belong to Chesterton. I have never heard Mr.

66

Darrow alone, but taken relatively, when that relativity is to Chesterton, he appears positively muddle-headed."

Although the terms of the debate were determined at the outset, Darrow either could not or would not stick to the definitions, but kept going off at illogical tangents and becoming choleric over points that were not in dispute. He seemed to have an idea that all religion was a matter of accepting Jonah's whale as a sort of luxury-liner. As Chesterton summed it up, he felt as if Darrow had been arguing all afternoon with his fundamentalist aunt, and the latter kept sparring with a dummy of his own mental making. When something went wrong with the microphone, Darrow sat back until it could be fixed. Whereupon G. K. C. jumped up and carried on in his natural voice, "Science you see is not infallible!" Whatever brilliance Darrow had in his own right, it was completely eclipsed. For all the luster that he shed, he might have been a remote star at high noon drowned by the bright incandescent arc light of the sun. Chesterton had the audience with him from the start, and when it was over, everyone just sat there, not wishing to leave. They were loath to let the light die!

Clarence Darrow wrote the author shortly before his death,

"I was favorably impressed by, warmly attached to, G. K. Chesterton. I enjoyed my debates with him, and found him a man of culture and fine sensibilities. If he and I had lived where we could have become better acquainted, eventually we would have ceased to debate, I firmly believe."

Bishop George Craig Stewart of Chicago, presided at Orchestra Hall when Chesterton debated in that city with Dr. Horace J. Bridges of the Ethical Cultural Society on the subject, "Is Psychology a Curse?" In his closing remarks Chesterton devastatingly sideswiped his opponent and wound up the occasion in a storm of laughter and applause,

"It is clear that I have won the debate, and we are all prepared to acknowledge that psychology is a curse. Let us, however, be magnanimous. Let us allow at least one person in this unhappy world to practice this cursed psychology, and I should like to nominate Dr. Bridges."

During Dr. Bridges' share of the debate Chesterton was drawing funny pictures on the back of a torn envelope which he produced out of his capacious inner pocket. At the close of the debate, Bishop Stewart begged the torn envelope with the funny pictures, which the artist initialed "From G. K.

68

C. to G. C. S." It now hangs framed
with one of G. K.'s photographs in the
episcopal drawingroom.

At luncheon Bishop Stewart remarked,
"Mr. Chesterton, **securus judicat orbis
terrarum.** You have become a Roman
Catholic, and I do not doubt that you
have gained the whole world, but may I
suggest that one may gain the whole
world and lose one's soul, and I think
you have lost the soul of Chestertonian-
ism, for after all, when you were an
Anglican you were both a Protestant
and a Catholic, and that was a delightfully Chestertonian position. Now you
have become a Romanist, you have
ceased to be a Chestertonian."

Chesterton's only response to this
Anglican leg pulling was a beaming and
chuckling acknowledgment of the
charge.

At the luncheon Chesterton talked
just as he wrote, on any subject that
came up, in a free, flowing, brilliant
manner, and everything he said might
have been taken down and published as
a part of his weekly letter to the
"Illustrated London News."

In introducing Chesterton for the debate, Bishop Stewart had quoted Oliver
Hereford's delightful verse,

"When plain folks such as you and I
See the sun sinking in the sky,
We think it is the setting sun:
But Mr. Gilbert Chesterton
Is not so easily misled;
He calmly stands upon his head,
And upside down obtains a new
And Chestertonian point of view..
Observing thus how from his nose
The sun creeps closer to his toes
He cries in wonder and delight,
How fine the sunrise is tonight!"

When the lecture was over, Chesterton strode down the aisle towards the main entrance where Mr. Edward Cassidy was standing with his wife who wished to get his autograph on a book. Suddenly a very important looking lorgnetted dowager accompanied by her daughter confronted the massive man.

"Mr. Chesterton," she demanded, "might I ask when did you become famous?"

"I became famous, if you can call it that," the great author chuckled, "at a time when there were no famous men in England."

He went on to explain that there had been no very great writers or journalists in England during the Boer War. His bitter opposition to the war ran so counter to the English press of the

70

period that he became famous for his
disloyalty, and for refusing to run with
the crowd.

Chesterton impressed the late Rev-
erend Frederic Seidenberg, S. J., who
was also present in Orchestra Hall, as
a man one could never forget, "not only
his huge size, but his striking personality and ever present smile are things
that one would carry through life. We
had a full house, but his voice was so
thin that I immediately had the speaker's desk placed at the edge of the foot-
lights. When he began again to speak
several in the balcony called out,
'Louder!' After a moment's hesitation,
Chesterton looked up and said, 'Good
brother, don't worry, you're not missing
a thing.' The audience roared."

Dr. Horace J. Bridges has kindly
given his impressions,

"I had two public debates with Chesterton, one in Chicago and one in Mil-
waukee. He struck me as a curious
mixture of great personal charm, wide
reading, exquisite critical faculty
(manifested particularly in his interpretations of Browning and of Dickens),
delightful humor, and a certain intellectual recklessness that made him in-
different to truth and reality. I cannot but feel that fundamentally—perhaps I should say subconsciously—he
was a thorough-going skeptic and acted

71

upon the principle that, since we cannot really be positive about anything, we had better believe what it pleases us to believe. I think he never did justice to the real arguments for a case he opposed; and he had a slap-dash way of assuming that the weaknesses in an opponent's case proved not only the falsity of that case, but—which is obviously a very different matter—the truth of his own case.

"One may think my criticism of him unfair. I certainly do not mean it to be so, nor do I fail to recognize that men much more earnest in their truth-seeking than he was have sincerely believed the things he said he believed. My comment is on his mental processes, in distinction from the question of his particular beliefs."

Chesterton spoke in St. Louis at the Odeon Theatre. On the stage his entire appearance was distinctive: shaggy, tousled dark-light hair topped a massive head and full, ruddy face; eyes which seemed always half-closed were protected by thick-lensed glasses; heavy shoulders and ponderous girth bulked above long, slender legs. Over evening dress he wore a black cape; when he doffed it and stood ready to speak, his stiff, white shirt-front became awry and crept several degrees out of proper position.

72

"A gentle giant Chesterton seemed," recalls Mr. James O'Neill, "as he commenced to address his audience. His high-pitched voice sounded somewhat of a plaintive and apologetic note." Lamenting the pseudo-sophistication of the day and the loss of appreciation for the simple pleasures of yore, Chesterton complained that the modern man and woman were seeking to escape ennui by finding new thrills, which tendency was expressed in our entertainments and even in our foods. Whereas we had once been satisfied with the taste of one palatable comestible at a time, we now demanded a combination of several in such an assembly as the modern three-deck sandwich. He regretfully observed that whereas our esthetic sense had once been pleased by such a dainty little figurine as the china shepherdess, we were now regaled by only such heroic figures as the billboard likeness of the lady who keeps her schoolgirl complexion by using a certain kind of soap and proclaims her secret to all who read. He was saddened by these thoughts and yearned for a return of the more simple but much more wholesome aesthetic attitudes currents in the days of his early manhood.

Mrs. Katharine Darst says that when there was a call for questions,

73

they were slow coming, and dull when
finally blurted out. Then there was a
long, embarrassing pause. And finally,
"Well, we've heard from the educated.
Now, have the ignorant anything to
ask?" . . . this from the Chairman.
Chesterton had such a vicious way of
tearing poseurs apart with his sharp
shafts that the reluctance of the audience to place itself at his mercy was
natural. But here was too good a
chance to miss. A number who had
hesitated to make inquiries were on
their feet at once. If they asked as
the ignorant, they felt that they were
armed against Chesterton's barbs!

A group of St. Louis women also
heard Chesterton deliver a lecture par-
adoxically entitled,

"The New Enslavement of Women."

This gave a compelling portrayal of
how women exchanged the freedom of
home for the slavery of office,

"Twenty million young women rose
to their feet with the cry, 'WE WILL
NOT BE DICTATED TO!' And immediately proceeded to become stenog-
raphers!"

# CHAPTER SEVEN

## SOME RECOLLECTIONS OF G. K. C.

Mr. Bernard Shaw told the author that he was so much struck by a review of Scott's "Ivanhoe" which appeared in the "Daily News" while Chesterton was holding his earliest notable job as feuilletonist to the paper that he wrote to him, "asking him who he was and where he came from, as he was evidently a new star in literature. He was either too shy or too lazy to answer. The next thing I remember is his lunching with us on quite intimate terms, accompanied by Belloc.

"Our actual physical contacts, however, were few, as he never belonged to the Fabian Society nor came to its meetings (this being my set) whilst his Fleet Street Bohemianism lay outside my vegetarian, teetotal, non-smoking tastes. Besides, he apparently liked literary society; and it had the grace to like him. I avoided it and it loathed me.

"But, of course, we were very conscious of one another. I enjoyed him and admired him keenly; and nothing could have been more generous than his treatment of me. Our controversies were exhibition spars, in which nothing could have induced either of us to hurt the other."

In July, 1933, the Canadian Authors' Association paying its first official visit to England, was entertained at Claridge's by the Royal Society of Literature. Miss Paty Carter recalls that at the end of the luncheon the toast was proposed by Rudyard Kipling and ably seconded by Chesterton. The contrast in appearance between the mover and seconder of the toast, caused a ripple of amusement: a contrast that might be likened to the Giant and Jack in the fairy story. Though Kipling, in reality, was only slightly below average size, and if a giant, Chesterton at least conveyed the impression of an amiable, gentle, likable giant.

"You will be much puzzled at my occupying any space—so much space— in this august assembly," he began, "and why any word of mine could possibly add to what this great literary genius, Mr Kipling, has said I cannot pose as a newspaper man; one reads of newspaper men slipping in through half-closed doors

"Now, no one could possibly think of me as slipping through a half-closed door! (Laughter).

"I do not know Canada as Mr. Kip-

76

ling knows it. I have traveled here and there in the miserable capacity of one giving lectures. I might call myself a lecturer; but then again I fear some of you may have attended my lectures. The reason for my presence here today is to return hospitality. I have been twice to Canada. My first visit was made twelve years ago when I crossed to the Dominion from America—that was in the early days of Prohibition. The second time I went up the St. Lawrence. Then I knew that Canada had the foundations of all literature, because she had indeed a country. There was that vast natural background necessary to the growth of literary culture, and there was also what is necessary for all literature—legend. On the Plains of Abraham I was uplifted in the sense in which poetry or great music or even a great monument uplifts one.

"The magnificent cordiality and courtesy of the Canadian people was, to me, amazing. The hospitality of the Canadian Authors' Association was overwhelming. The Canadian Literature Society rushed out to welcome any stray traveler, and in the confusion I was mistaken for a literary man. (Laughter). I tried to explain I was merely a lecturer, and one of the first things for a lecturer to do is talk about

77

things he does not understand, such as Canada."

"Are you coming with us to Downing Street, Mr. Chesterton?" asked Miss Carter as the authors all left the hotel.

"No—o," he drawled, with a delicious sort of chant. "Unfortunately, I have to attend a wretched meeting with three other men; all madmen, like myself!"

Mr. James Truslow Adams happened to have been one of the four or five Americans elected to the Royal Society of Literature, and so he found himself in the rather odd situation of an American who was entertaining Canadians at an empire meeting.

"Chesterton," recalls Mr. Adams, "was very witty, and although he took a number of sharp cracks at American journalism, I being the only person in the room who was not of the British Empire, there was nothing untrue or unkind. I have an extremely vivid impression of the man, not only of his enormous physical bulk and of his constant mopping of his forehead with his handkerchief, but also of his intellectual vitality."

The President of the Canadian Authors' Association, the late Charles W. Gordon (Ralph Connor) was "struck with the freshness of Chesterton's thought, the brilliancy of his imagination, and his warm human sympathy. I had heard him spoken of as cold, but I could not say that of his speech or of his personality that day."

Mr. Rodolphe L. Megroz made a pilgrimage in 1922, to Chesterton's home.

"Oh, yes, certainly, sir," said the railway porter at Beaconsfield when asked where Chesterton lived. "Turn to your left at the bridge and along the road to the old town. When you come to the film studios, go across into the side road and it's surrounded by a field. His house is called 'Top Meadow'."

Mr. and Mrs. Chesterton received the visitor in a little room with whitewashed walls and book-cases, and a long desk below a window that ran the length of the room. Megroz was anxious to compare Chesterton's ideas with those of H. G. Wells whom he had seen shortly before, and particularly wished to question the former's opinions on patriotism and nationalism. Although such books as the jolly "Napoleon of Notting Hill" belonged to the pre-war period, G. K. C.'s own journalistic writings had shown no change in his dislike of internationalism and the kind of social organization favored by Wells.

"The trouble is," he said, "that terms like patriotism and nationalism are very often used by people who mean something quite different from what I mean.

My idea in 'The Napoleon of Notting Hill' was that men have a natural loyalty for their own home and their own land, I do not see why, instead of progress lying in the direction of bigger and bigger everything, it should not be found in the opposite direction, in local patriotism. I say let a man go on loving his own home, he will all the better recognize the other fellow's right to do so."

"H. G. Wells," continued Chesterton, "talks about abstractions like the World State, which has no root. The League of Nations lost its grip on realities by ignoring local patriotism."

When Megroz repeated Chesterton to H. G. Wells the latter remarked,

"Possibly the World State is an abstraction at present, but what are not abstractions are the flying machines and poison gas; electricity and wireless; the fact that the food grown in India may be eaten in England, and the food grown in Australia may be eaten at the Cape. These are hard facts, and they demand sane treatment as hard facts, and the only possible sane treatment is to bring them under one comprehensive control."

Megroz got the impression that Chesterton was "certainly a romanticist, often escaping from reality. By fantasies, among which may be included

his medievalism; but always one comes
back to his great sanity, his poetic insight, his sweetness which redeemed
all his propaganda, illuminated his
poetry, and could fill even the detective
story with a wisdom akin to mysticism."
What Chesterton wrote his friend
Mr. W. R. Titterton about Wells is per-
tinent, and is here published for the
first time, and with Mr. Wells' leave,

My dear Titterton:

I think we might drop the formal address on both sides; especially as I
want to write to you about a personal
feeling which I don't want you to take
too officially, or in that sense too seriously. I ought to have written direct
to Pugh to thank him for his great
generosity in giving us his most interesting sketch about Wells, which you
were good enough to arrange for us.
My task is made a little more delicate
now, because there is something I feel
about it, which I do hope neither he nor
you would exaggerate or misunderstand.
I was the more glad of his kind offer,
when he made it, because I thought nobody could more ably and sincerely appreciate Wells; and I was rather pleased
that Wells should be appreciated in a
paper where he had been so often crit-
icized. I do hope this work will not
turn into anything that looks like a

mere attack on Wells; especially in the rather realistic and personal modern manner, which I am perhaps too Victorian myself to care very much about. I do not merely feel this because I have managed to keep Wells as a friend on the whole. I feel it much more (and I know you are a man to understand such sentiments) because I have a sort of sense of honor about him as an enemy, or at least a potential enemy. We are so certain to collide in controversial warfare, that I have a horror of his thinking I would attack him with anything but fair controversial weapons. My feeling is so entirely consistent with a faith in Pugh's motives, as well as an admiration of his talents, that I honestly believe I could explain this to him without offense; and I will if necessary write to him to do so; but I thought I would write to you first; as you know him and may possibly know his aims and attitude as I do not.

I am honestly in a very difficult position on the "New Witness," because it is physically impossible for me really to edit it, and also do enough outside work to be able to edit it unpaid, as well as having a little over to give to it from time to time. What we should have done without the loyalty and capacity of you and a few others I can't imagine. I cannot oversee everything

82

that goes into the paper and it would certainly be most uncomfortable for either of us to exercise our rights of "cutting" stuff given to us under such circumstances as Pugh's: but I think I should exercise it if Pugh went very far in the realistic manner about some of the weak points in Wells' career. There were one or two phrases about old quarrels in the last number which strike a note I should really regret touching more serious things; and I should like to consult with you about such possibilities before they appear in the paper. I cannot do it with most things in the paper, as I say; and nobody could possibly do it better than you. On the other hand, I cannot resign, without dropping, as you truly say, the work of a great man who is gone; and who, I feel, would wish me to continue it. It is like what Stevenson said about Marriage and its duties: "There is no refuge for you; not even suicide." But I should have to consider even resignation, if I felt that the acceptance of Pugh's generosity really gave him the right to print something that I really felt bound to disapprove. It may be that I am needlessly alarmed over a slip or two of the pen, in vivid descriptions of a very odd character; and that Pugh really admires his Big Little H. G. as I thought he did at the beginning of the business. I only write this to confide to you what is in my mind, which is far from an easy task; but I think you are one to understand. If the general impression on the reader's mind is of the Big Wells and not the little Wells, I think the doubt I mean would really be met.

Yours always sincerely,<br>G. K. Chesterton.

Mr. Titterton wrote in a letter a few years ago:

"Edward Macdonald assists G. K. C. in editing the 'Rag.' In fact he does all the technical editing, though G. K. C. controls the strategy. He is a splendid fellow, very simple and humble, very loyal, very wise. His editing of "G. K.'s Weekly" is a labor of love. What I know of G. K. you know already. You must be with him day by day to see the infinite simplicity—innocence —and friendliness of the man. We are fortunate to be led by a little child. When we were starting the Distributist League, I suggested that it should be called 'The League of the Little Man.' And G. K. C. said that, though he liked the title, he thought that, with him as President, it would be regarded as a great joke. Probably it would have been. Yet, in fact, he IS the little Man."

Mr. Hugo C. Riviere has pleasant recollections of having painted Chesterton's portrait:
"What excellent talk I heard when he
was sitting to me. It was, as I so often
saw him, in his big Inverness cape with
that massive head at that time covered
with a big mane of brown hair, his hat
on the grass and a favorite sword stick
brandished against the sky. It was just
after his 'Napoleon of Notting Hill'
was written. A little later I was to be
made a very proud man by receiving a
copy of 'The Flying Inn' and finding it
was dedicated to me. You know, of
course, what a fine large style G. K. C.
had himself as a draughtsman with a
great and free grasp of form and character. How often when dining with us
I have seen him take out an old envelope and rapidly cover it with extraordinary sketches. I have one carefully
treasured in my 'Napoleon of Notting
Hill' an old envelope covered with every
sort and type of hand and figure, some
in medieval dress, and some modern,
two or three clever heads of G. B. Shaw
and other clerical and political and im-
aginary. How delightful were the illustrations he made for 'The Biography
of Beginners' that he and E. C. Bentley
did together. I also remember G. K. C.,
after writing an article, over his last
glass of wine when all of us, and he too,

85

were talking after dinner, and the boy sent by whatever magazine it was destined for, waiting in the hall. His favorite, and I think, characteristic, taste in wine was red Burgundy, but he did not notice his food much, as he was far too busy thinking and talking."

Mr. Hermon Ould, the Secretary-General of the P. E. N. Club, met Chesterton many times. When H. G. Wells found the presidency too onerous and was threatening to resign, Mr. Ould offered the office to Chesterton who replied in a characteristic letter, dated August 2, 1935:

Dear Mr. Ould:

"You might imagine how miserable I feel in having again delayed a reply to your kind letters; and being again, after a struggle, forced back on the same dismal reply. The truth is that I did very much wish to accept this great distinction you have offered me; and have been trying to think of various ways in which it might be managed; but have come back to the conclusion that it really cannot be managed. The delay was partly due to your own persuasive powers; for I must admit that I was a good deal shaken by what you said about the possibilities of using the position for many things in which I believe. If I may say so, you

86

must be a very good secretary; and a good secretary is much more important than a good president. But I am practically certain that I should not be a good president. I am honestly thinking in the interests of the Club; and I feel it would be better for me to decline the candidature than for me to resign rather abruptly soon afterwards, because I found the responsibilities you describe too incompatible with the responsibilities I have already. As you truly say, it would be unworthy to accept what is merely a sinecure; and I really cannot manage this additional cure of souls . . . .

Yours faithfully,<br>
G. K. Chesterton.

Father Vincent C. Donovan spent a good part of an afternoon with Chesterton and his wife at Boston's Chatham Hotel. Many things were discussed, but Father Donovan recalls that the visitors were particularly interested in their impressions of America. They found Boston very English in appearance and atmosphere. Among other things Chesterton said,

"All the Jews have been hounding me as a result of my 'New Jerusalem.' I am not a little hurt and puzzled about their unreasonable attitude because in that work I have honestly tried to be objective, fair, and understanding, but they won't see that."

Mr. Vincent de Paul Fitzpatrick first met Chesterton at the Belvedere Hotel, Baltimore, in February, 1921, and recalls that he praised the persistency of the Irish in struggling for their rights:

"When you hear of an organization in England fighting for liberty, you must find whether or not that organization contains much Irish blood. It means all the difference in the world. If you hear in this country of a strike in the Cycle Valley, it is nothing to get worried over. But if you hear of a strike in Glasgow, you may expect something exclusive and exciting. The reason is that a mass of the Irish poor is found in that city, and the Irish will not submit meekly when any person or any group tries to trample upon them..

"We see the English people grumbling at the perpetual interference with their rights and at the various restricitons to which they are subjected, but they are not organized. There are plenty of old radicals in England, who, as individuals, are sincere defenders of liberty, but they are isolated. Take, for example, old Dr. Johnson. With the Irish Catholics things are different. Their love for liberty seems to have been created by the Catholic Church—

their only corporate defender of liberty
today—is the Catholic Church. Liberty
means much to her—something to be
protected. She defends it with her powerful organization. When we speak of
the English Labor party in England
fighting for its rights, we do not mean
the English labor party, at all, we mean
the Scotch-Irish Labor party."

On December 7, 1930, Mr. Fitzpatrick
had a long talk with Chesterton at the
St. Moritz, New York City. It was the
eve of the feast of the Immaculate Conception, and Chesterton was thinking of
his newly found Faith,

"It stands to reason that Christmas
means more to me now that I am a
Catholic than it did befire I was con-
verted to the Faith. But Christmas has
meant much to me ever since my boyhood. I believed in Christmas before I
believed in Christ. In the years immediately before my conversion I naturally thought much more seriously about
Christmas, my thoughts became more
consoling and Christmas was more
beautiful as the passing days drew me
nearer to the Church.

"I believed in the spirit of Christmas
and I liked Christmas, even when I was
a boy filled with radicalistic tendencies
when I really thought I was atheistic.
In those days I wrote a poem to the
Blessed Virgin. I was quite young and

89

the poem, God help me, must have
been a rather wretched thing, though
I imitated Swinburne, or at least, tried
to imitate him when I wrote it.

"From my early years I had an affection for the Blessed Virgin and for
the Holy Family. The story of Bethle-
hem and the story of Nazareth appealed
to me deeply when I was a boy. Long
before I joined the Catholic Church the
Immaculate Conception had my allegiance. That allegiance has been inten-
sified steadily..

"Aside from the teaching of the
Church on the subject, a doctrine which
we as Catholics accept, the thought that
there was in all the ages one creature,
and that creature a woman, who was
preserved from the slightest taint of
sin, won my heart."

Mother Mary St. Luke recalls that
during Chesterton's visit to Rome in
the late Autumn of 1929, he went several times to the Convent of the Holy
Child, where he lectured one day before
a crowded audience on "Thomas Moore
and Humanism." At the conclusion,
a Father Cuthbert thanked the speaker
and expressed the appreciation of the
audience, remarking on the mental re-
semblance of More and Chesterton, saying that he could quite well imagine
them sitting together making jokes,

some of them VERY good, and some of them VERY bad.

The Chestertons were also present in the Vatican at the reading of the Degree for the Beatification of the English Martyrs. At the conclusion of the ceremony there was the usual rush and confusion in the neighborhood of the cloak-room next to the sala Clementina. A group of Holy Child pupils having gathered around Chesterton, and learned of his dismay at not being able to retrieve his famous cloak from the "Bussolanti" on account of the milling crowd, plunged into the melee and brought it back to him in triumph. They also secured a taxi for them in the Piazza di San Pietro—no small feat on such an occasion! G. K. expressed his appreciation of their efforts in his own beautiful "architectural" handwriting, which constitutes one of the most treasured possessions of the school,

"For the Young Ladies Suffering Education at the Convent of the Holy Child.

"To be a Real Prophet once
For you alone did I desire,
Who dragged the Prophet's Mantle down
And brought the Chariot of Fire."

91

# CHAPTER EIGHT

## CHESTERTON AT NEW HAVEN

Thomas Caldecot Chubb met Chesterton at the Elizabethan Club in New Haven almost twenty years ago, and his initial impression still persists that he was a large man in every way, "Physically, of course, he was the size of Falstaff, but that is not all I am talking about. Perhaps the best way of saying what I mean, is to point out that he had this further in common with the huge knight who is, in a sense, truly Shakespeare's most tragic figure: that beneath surface-wit and brilliance there was something one must label deep and profound."

Chesterton had been lecturing to a typical Yale audience of the early '20's —four or five consciously literary undergraduates who made a grim duty of never missing such a talk, and about ninety percent of the membership of the local women's clubs. The Speaker spilled over, like a wine keg broached, into the Middle Ages. Among other things, he spoke, naturally, of their individual craftsmanship. He related how it appeared even in such matters as meat and drink. He regretted with a nostalgic gusto those gone days when, as he put it, every monastery, almost every home had its own brand of liqueur or wine. Then he was transported from the crowded hall with its murmurs of polite, not too comprehending, applause, and made to stand in the dark living room of the white building across the street, with its comfortable shabby leather chairs, and its stiff painting of an acidulous and very white-faced Virgin Queen; and as he stood there— wearing a grey suit (so the picture, though perhaps inaccurately after so long a time, comes back to Chubb) and holding a cup of tea in one hand, his eyeglasses in the other—Chubb was introduced to him.

"Mr. Chesterton," Chubb said, "you have your wish."

Obviously, he wanted to know what wish and how he had it.

"Thanks to Prohibition, every house is making, if not its own liqueur, at least its own likker."

It cannot truthfully be related that he was hugely diverted by Chubb's attempt at being facetious. Bathtub gin was, it may be supposed, hardly just the evocation he would have wished of the spirit of the age of Abelard and Aquinas. And furthermore, Prohibition was a serious matter, not a jesting one. So

Chubb was properly covered with an appropriate undergraduate confusion which he tried to hide by holding out a copy of "The Ballad of the White Horse." This haltingly—after his previous boldness—he asked him to autograph and to write a verse from it upon the fly-leaf.

"There is no need to go into details about his courteous compliance other than to indicate the thrill it gave me," recollects Chubb, "by saying that in that varnished period the 'Ballad' seemed to me a high point in English poetry. It seemed almost incredible I was actually talking to and facing the man who wrote it. But a confession must be added to this statement. It was virtually all of Chesterton I knew by having read. That and 'Lepanto' were the only Chestertonian works I had deigned to cast my eyes upon. Of course, I knew the names of others. But that anyone who could write this immortal stuff should waste his time turning out such poor trash as a series of fluent novels, certain aggravating essays, a contradicting sort of history of England, and—horror of horrors — the Father Brown 'detective' stories, was, in a ghastly way, incredible. It was potboiling. It was prostituting one's genius. It was selling out to Mammon and the Philistines. And that was, of course, the sin against the Holy Ghost.

"It is now necessary to reverse that stand—though here perhaps youth's headlong egotism has merely been replaced by incipient middle age's complacent one. For somehow the swinging lines which relate Alfred's adventures seem a little bouncy now. They are dated, just as a brass radiator and acetylene lamps would date even a T-model Ford. Even the young don't turn to them, being engaged in writing not quite grammatical verses to Communism and proletarian poetry which no member of the proletariat can make head or tail of. And 'Lepanto,' which —with 'Ivry' and what Tennyson has to say about the Revenge—is among the most stirring short narrative poetry of the language, does not set the pulses beating quite as rapidly in 1939 as it did in 1922. But the entertainment and wisdom of 'The Flying Inn,' 'The Man Who Was Thursday,' and 'The Napoleon of Notting Hill,' and the cool, paradoxical truths—well, anyway, from time to time they are true—of the essays, of the history, of the writing on Browning, Thackeray and Dickens, of the controversies with that irritating but likeable friend-adversary G. B. S., still have their power to stimulate. And personally I now believe that the best of Chesterton can be found, if you delve for it, in the Father Brown stories; that out of them can be mined by an attentive prospector the purest Chestertonian gold.

"All of which, if true, places the man for us. A stimulating writer, a delightful writer, on certain occasions even an important writer, but was he quite a great one? With Kipling, Wells, Shaw, Arnold Bennett and perhaps half a dozen others with whom I will not rashly provoke controversy by naming, he will be compulsory reading for every student of the era. It is less certain that the general public will turn to him after a hundred or even after fifty years.

"Yet he has given a lot, and in no way more than by his provocative way of seeing and saying things. He loves Meredith and he hates Hardy, yet he nails truth to the wall by saying that the man of the two who had a healthy point of view had the perverse and crabbed style, whereas the one with the perverse and crabbed point of view had the healthy and manly style. He stated pungently and accurately—writing of 'The Book of Snobs'—that 'aristocracy does not have snobs any more than democracy does.' Thackeray might have learned something from this. He had the insight to realize that Browning was among the finest love poets of the world though quite to the contrary runs the general opinion. (A similar, though not the same, revolutionary statement might be made of our own E. A. Robinson, substituting perhaps emotion for love.) He considered—a half truth—that the whole of present day England was the remains of Rome; and—a whole truth—that Henry VIII was as unlucky in his wives as they were in him. Which statements, plucked very haphazardly from out of his writings, ought to indicate what I mean."

Another who heard him at Yale was Mr. Harold Chapman Bailey:

"Chesterton's lecture, as I recall it, was given in the Sprague Memorial Hall, which is part of the Yale Music School. The entire subject matter of the Chesterton address has escaped me, but in the question period afterward the first two or three questions were so puerile that despite my youth I was emboldened to rise with this query: 'Will you not tell me something about William Cobbett?'

"I recall that at first Mr. Chesterton did not understand my question, but when I repeated it, he seemed greatly pleased to find that in far away America there was some interest in Cobbett. Accordingly he spent at least five min-

97

utes explaining to us who William Cobbett was, what he stood for, and how in a measure Cobbett was his own spiritual ancestor. He concluded by remarking that the Yale University Press would do well to get out a new edition of Cobbett's works. I have often wondered whether this query of mine played any part in stimulating him later on to write a volume on Cobbett."

Major James B. Pond also met G. K. C. at New Haven, and had the privilege of being present when Chesterton and 'A. E.' (George Russell) met at the William Lyon Phelps' house in New Haven. It was the first time these two men ever met. Russell hardly ever went out of Ireland and these two famous men had to come to New Haven to get personally acquainted. It happened they were both lecturing the same day.

# CHAPTER NINE

## AT NOTRE DAME.

Chesterton was guest lecturer at Notre Dame University for the first semester of the 1930-1 school year, delivering eighteen lectures on English history, and the same number on the Victorian age of English literature.

Visiting Beaconsfield a few years ago, Father John F. O'Hara, President of the University, told Chesterton that he had received "numerous letters from former students who were just beginning to appreciate the lectures he had given them. Chesterton was that way. One was forced to remember his striking sentences, and the underlying truth forced itself on the mind of the undergraduate when greater experience made understanding possible."

As Chesterton walked out on the stage and faced his first Notre Dame audience, he leaned upon the lectern and said, "Until quite recently, I was not at all certain that I would be able to be here tonight. Had I not come, you would now be gazing upon a great yawning void instead of myself."

This bit of humor and the manner in which it was expressed gave Father Charles Morton the feeling that here was a man of rare humility and of the simplicity which always accompanies genuine culture. As the lecture series progressed, two other qualities became prominent,—brilliance of mind and a profound Catholic faith. No matter what the subject of his lecture was, whether in the field of literature or of history, he invariably found a way at the end to relate all he had said to some profound religious truth. That people should praise him as a learned man was a source of genuine embarrassment to him. It amused him to be addressed as "professor," and he invariably referred to himself as a "mere journalist."

Father Patrick J. Carroll looked upon Chesterton, master of antithesis "as himself the antithesis. A large lumbering hulk of a man, you would expect from him a deep, thundering speech. You are mistaken: his language is swift, sudden, arresting. Epigram follows epigram, until you get tired of brilliance, and begin to wonder if this big man is not more concerned with his sword play than with the serious business of defending truth against truth's enemies. That is how you sometimes think: but, of course, your thinking is wrong."

Prof. Norbert Engels of the College of Arts and Sciences recalls that "at every lecture knowledge poured forth.

He never used a paper, a note, or a reference of any kind. He would quote extremely long passages of poetry or prose with utmost ease. I did not tire of his use of paradox as he used it with such consummate art. Those are inadequate judges of his genius who pronounce upon him from his writings only. To know Chesterton fully, besides his works, one should have heard him lecture, in order to catch the spirit of the man."

All the breath and flavor of ages of Christian culture came with Chesterton in the opinion of Father Charles M. Carey, "he entered our campus like some great Catholic warrior stepping down from the centuries that date back to a time when England was really 'Merrie England.' Huge in girth and mind and heart, he was the embodiment of all that was good in that splendid Catholic heritage.

"As his vast physical bulk lumbered from the wings to the rostrum, then slouched down in his chair, he threw a ruddy scowl across the rows of young University men before him, and a great feeling of awe swallowed up the idle chatter. There was not a single heart in that young Catholic audience that did not somehow experience the presence of greatness in our midst. To the man who knew little of the great apol-

101

ogist, it may have been a moment of confused terror and curiosity. To anyone who had read but a paragraph from his pen, it was the moment which finds one helplessly silent in the presence of a superior being.

" 'So,' I thought to myself, as Chesterton thundered and swayed slightly to his place, his bushy hair in its own convenient parting and his wrinkled and baggy clothing left to look after itself with a pronounced abandon, 'can this be the man that is so mentally nimble, so sure footed in thought, so precise in diction, so accurate in his thrusts, so merciless in heaping wrath on adversaries, and so loud in his frequent laughter at the absurdity of those who oppose his Christian fighting?' "

Once he began to speak, Chesterton's eyes lit up with a joy born of that common bond that is the Catholic faith, thus destroying all barriers of racial differences because, as he said, "Under the portals of our Lady's Shrine, all men are at home." That was the spirit that characterized his stay at Notre Dame. To his young listeners he was an inspiration. Every word that he uttered had a clear, certain and convincing ring in it that made for conviction. He was thoroughly Catholic. For him life was full of faith and beauty and romance. Every word that he uttered had a freshness and wonder about it. His adroit phraseology, his accent and his inexhaustible flow of genuine humor quickened his youthful audience to frequent bursts of applause and measured gaiety.

Chesterton had the honorary degree of Doctor of Law conferred upon him Wednesday afternoon, November 5, 1930, in Washington Hall. Many honorary degrees had been conferred by Notre Dame, but this was the first time in the history of the University that a special convocation of the Faculty had been called to participate in the conferring of a degree.

At four-thirty the academic procession left the University parlors and made its way to Washington Hall where members of the Senior Class and the guests were assembled. After an introductory musical program had been given by the student orchestra and Glee Club, Father J. Leonard Carrice, Director of Studies, announced the conferring of the degree,

"The University of Notre Dame, in this special convocation of the Faculty, confers the degree of Doctor of Law, **honoris causa**, on a man of letters recognized as the ablest and most influential in the English-speaking world of today, a defender of the Christian tradition, whose keen mind, right heart,

103

and versatile literary genius have been valiantly devoted to eternal truth, goodness and beauty, in literature, and in life—Gilbert Keith Chesterton, of London, England.

After receiving the Degree from Notre Dame's President, the Rev. Charles L. O'Donnell, Doctor Chesterton replied,

"I only wish it were possible for me to say, as you have suggested, something of what is in my heart in the way of gratitude. Gratitude is what I feel most deeply at present, and it is the irony of human fate that it is perhaps the only thing that cannot be expressed. If I said all the things which are usually said on these occasions, I should only be expressing my feelings, for in my case, they happen to be perfectly true. It is usual to say that one is not worthy of such an honor, and the vividness of my own unworthiness is so acute in my own mind that I find it almost impossible to express it and to thank you for the far too generous things which have been said. I have given a series of lectures on a subject on which a number of you are much better acquainted than I. If I happen to say something about the history of the Victorian age, the history which I am supposed to talk about, or if I happen to say something about the Victorian age in literature, I am all too painfully reminded that you have learned history and have studied literature. If I mention the Province of Canada, I am reminded that you have studied geography. Therefore I am afraid that I am not only unworthy but almost in a false position before you. I am a journalist, and the one thing I can claim is that I have endeavored to show that it is possible to be an honest journalist. Therefore, a great academic distinction of this kind gives me a very strong sense of gratitude. I can only thank you from the bottom of my heart, not only for this favor extended to me, but also for the very great patience with which you have listened to my lectures.

"There is always a bond between us that would make you tolerant of me, I know. I have only once before gone through a ceremony of this kind and that was at the highly Protestant University of Edinburgh, where I found that part of the ceremony consisted of being lightly touched on the head with the cap of John Knox. I was very much relieved to find that it was not part of the ceremony on the present occasion that I should, let us say, wear the hat of Senator Heflin! I remember that, when I came to America before, about nine years ago, when I was not a catholic, and when I had hardly realized

105

that there were Catholics in America, my first sensation in this country was one of terror. I recall the first landing and that great hotel in New York, the Biltmore, the name of which held for me such terrifying possibilities. (Surely there would not be **more** of it!) It all seemed alien, although I quickly discovered what kind and generous people the Americans are. I did not feel at all like that when I came to America for the second time. If you want to know why I felt different, the reason is in the name of your University. That name was quite sufficient as far as I was concerned. I would not have mattered if it had been in the mountains of the moon. Wherever She has erected Her pillars, all men are at home, and I knew that I should not find strangers. And, if any of you who are young should go to other countries, you will find that what I have said is true."

Prof. Daniel O'Grady was invited to a social evening with Chesterton at Notre Dame's Sorin Hall . . . among those present were the host Charles Philips, Paul Fenlon, Pat Manion, John Frederick, Lee Flateley, John Connolly, Steve Roney, Rufus Rauch . . . all either professors or students. The affair started at nine in the evening and lasted until almost three in the morning.

When Manion asked whether liquor

in England produced immorality, G. K. C. replied,

"Undoubtedly it does in certain London districts. When I stayed at the Royal York in Toronto on my way down to Notre Dame I noticed something oligarchical about the Ontario system inasmuch as there was a dance on and those who could afford a room left the ballroom on occasion and went upstairs for a nip displaying visible evidences thereof as one met them in the hall. Moreover in Ontario a permit was necessary whereas in Catholic Quebec this Protestant condition did not prevail."

"I live near Oxford, and I often visit friends there. In Cambridge too I know and admire many men, such as the poet A. E. Housman, and the historians George M. Trevelyan and Holland Rose, the great Napoleonic authority. Speaking of the latter place you know the old yarn about the Italian doctor on his way to Cambridge to debate some don there. On stopping to inquire directions of some pedestrians he was answered in Greek verse by Cambridge students disguised as workmen, whereupon he ordered the coachman to turn around and go back because said he, if the laborers are so learned, what must the dons be? . . ."

When O'Grady said he had heard that

the difference between the two schools was that an Oxford man went around as though he owned the place, while a Cambridge man acted as though he didn't give a damn who did, Chesterton retorted,

"And both about equally obnoxious!"

When the discussion turned to some well known Englishmen, Chesterton said,

"If my description of Lord Beaverbrook was based on his journalistic methods I would have to call him a guttersnipe. I feel that Bertrand Russell is a disgrace to English literature, not only on account of his writings, but also because of his way of life."

"Masefield's a fine fellow and a good writer," said Chesterton in reply to another question, "but Ramsay MacDonald had to choose Masefield as Poet Laureate, there being no other post so sympathetic to Labor. However, Yeats was by far our best poet. Yet hardly ever has the best poet been made laureate. There is too much politics in the appointment, just as is the case with the appointment of the Anglican bishops. One need only consider Barnes of Birmingham. The idea of calling York's archbishop 'by divine permission' and Canterbury's 'by divine consent,' has always seemed to me rather farfetched."

When reference was made to Rebecca West's resigning from the "Bookman" because the editorial policy favored the New Humanists, Chesterton remarked,

"How extremely foolish that is—as though that affected your contributions!"

Asked about Lord Beaverbrook who had but recently died, Chesterton reflected,

"Birkenhead has always been a puzzle to me because he was cynical and worldly ambitiouus, and yet, it must be confessed, overfond of his liquor. One expects such a weakness only from a poet or one who has the poetical imagination."

A comparison being made between certain types of Russian and English characters, Chesterton went on to say,

"The Russians in their writings are always brooding over fate or some silly thing. For the most part the English gentry are fine, sensible fellows, although, of course, there are some bounders amongst them. You will now find not a few Catholics among them, although for many years the only Catholics were either English aristocrats or Irish paupers."

Asked if he found the Americans all very mad in the pursuit of money, he shook his head with a smile,

"Quite the contrary, I find the Americans less worshipful of money than my fellow English. However, I do prefer even our English gentry although mad about money, to some of your vulgar and blatant millionaires."

During a discussion of the Church and State, Chesterton remarked,

"I read the other day of a western magistrate who sentenced a woman to go to Church for the next fifty Sundays. I wondered at the time whether that was consistent with the American doctrine of the separation of Church and State. Even though we have a state church in England, I do not think that an English judge would have given such a sentence."

In autographing a book just before the party broke up, Chesterton threw a lot of ink on the floor, but merely remarked,

"I'm always cluttering up people's carpets."

His hostess rather prim and proper, kept shoving ash-trays at him which he completely ignored and continued dropping ashes from his cigarettes all over the floor. But no one minded this little thoughtlessness of genius.

As he put on his Inverness cape and black sombrero-like hat he shouted out in merry tones,

"If anyone ever tries to tell me

110

Catholicism is inconsistent with fun and play, I'll say did you ever hear of the University of Notre Dame?"

Before Chesterton left the University, Mr. William L. Piedmont had a pleasant chat with him. Asked what he thought of our great American sports, G. K. C. answered,

"I witnessed the Notre Dame-Navy game, and was much impressed by the popularity that your game of football enjoys. In my youth I played English football and even rounders which might be described as an English equivalent of baseball."

"I very gravely doubt if the nations are becoming closer and closer together," declared Chesterton when the conversation touched the League of Nations. "Quite the contrary, I feel the various countries are becoming more national. An example would be in the literary fact that in my youth Thoreau, Hawthorne, Mark Twain and the rest were as widely known and read in Europe as in America, while today the strange and awful stuff of American writers is unknown abroad with very few exceptions. I attribute this to the fact that America has become so different and in Europe the news hasn't gotten through yet as to what it's all about in America."

On being asked if he thought the

111

world (and especially, the United States) possessed any great thinkers, he replied humorously,

"If there are any people in the world today who do think, witness my 'Age of Unreason,' I feel America can certainly claim some of them."

After confessing that he read very few novels, but mentioning the works of Sheila Kaye-Smith with approbation, he went on to say,

"But I consider Rebecca West the most interesting woman writer, if for no other reason than because she is gradually becoming more respectable. I suppose (with a characteristic chuckle) that her marrying a banker is not really the cause of respectability, even though marrying a banker may be a sort of worldly parallel to being confirmed in grace!"

Of the winner of the Nobel prize for literature, he said,

"On the whole, I think Sinclair Lewis is the scourge of God—a calamity in some respects like the Great Fire of London. I do not believe that Mr. Lewis has enough sympathy with the Middle West people of whom he writes, nor has he the right slant on the people of Main Street—as I have observed them during my sojourn in America. I think it about time somebody made fun of the greasy optimism prevalent

112

in recent novels. Lewis has a good
deal of righteous indignation, but what
he lacks is the positive moral idea
which should be found in the represen-
tative literature of every nation. I like
Lewis when he is simply humorous like
in "The Man Who Knew Coolidge," but
in general the bestowal of the prize is
like giving a medal to a great scaven-
ger."

When he arrived in Washington, D. C.
to lecture at Trinity College, Chesterton
gave Miss Syd Walsh an interesting and
picturesque description of Notre Dame,

"I think the faculty and students
awfully jolly people and the campus
itself a bit of medievalism with its constant stream of youths in bright colors
pouring in and out of old stone build-
ings with gilded domes. As long as I
live I will never forget their way of
letting off fireworks before a big game
and generally playing the goat in a
cheery way."

113

Greetings to the Mark Twain
Society —
from an Innocent at Home

R. Chesterton

known as the Unjumping
Frog of Bucks County.

and from Frances Chesterton
wife of the Innocent —
Aug. 1930

Top Meadow
Beaconsfield.

FACSIMILE WRITING
of
MR. AND MRS. G. K. CHESTERTON

114

CHAPTER TEN

## CHESTERTON AND AMERICAN
## AUTHORS.

Recently there appeared a statement to the effect that although Chesterton had considerable popularity with the average American reader, our authors cared but little for the man and his work. Doubting such a sweeping statement, I wrote to various men of letters who would serve as a good cross-section of American literature, and their replies proved unusually illuminating.

"Of course you may put me down as an admirer of Chesterton," declares Channing Pollock," though I recall surprisingly little of his work. I have read so much that, after fifty-six years, I begin to find recollections blurred. My admiration of Chesterton is founded on my impression of the man—of what he was and stood for; of his sincerity, courage, forthrightness and general altruism."

"As a boy of ten," records Thomas O. Mabbott, "I read regularly copies of the 'London Illustrated News' to which G. K. C. was a regular contributor. I

115

am one of those people who, while not exactly a prodigy, developed very early and think very much more as I did when sixteen than most people seem to do. I often boast how little most writers influence my own thought but Chesterton is one of the few who did! I read much of his work as a very young man, and believe he is one of the very few authors who impressed me **profoundly.** I saw 'Magic' when it was given in New York during the war—a mark of devotion, surely, since I rarely went to a serious play. Incidentally I thought it **very** effective as an acted play."

Clement Wood first read "Heretics" and then "Orthodoxy," and immediately obtained the impression that the author was "one of the world's most alert and persuasively brilliant minds. He made the persons treated of real and significant to me for the first time. Thereafter I read most of his work. His novels are absolutely unique, I wouldn't be without one, and of all, the 'Napoleon of Notting Hill' is the most precious— the glorious effort to revive medievalism today (which I am 100% against intellectually) won me forever. His Father Brown stories, in spite of the ever - present propaganda for Catholicism—which again I am against, but I believe that if religion persists, it will

116

either be Roman Catholic or the Quaker non-Christian (Religious Society of Friends) non-evangelical faith—I regard as by all odds the greatest detective stories ever written. Poe and Doyle are forerunners, and then G. K. C. whose every word is a work of art. I have memorized the plots of nearly all and the wording of many of his memorable openings. His 'Peacock Trees,' 'Club of Queen Trades,' rank as highly.

"The play 'Magic' is immortal and weighs more to me than all Shaw!"

"You may certainly enroll me as one of his admirers," affirms Donald Ogden Stewart. "Although I do not recall the name of the first book of his which I read, I do remember, however, that it was while I was in my senior year at Yale, and that it had such an influence on me that I immediately proceeded to read every one of his books that I could lay my hands on."

Henry Hazlitt first encountered Chesterton's writings in 1916 and "was quickly carried away by his stylistic brilliance. My admiration, I must confess, was not sustained at its original level, but it most certainly never deserted me. I never met him personally, but I heard him debate with Clarence Darrow, and was impressed by his im-

117

mense superiority over his antagonist, and by his charm as a man."

William Thomas Walsh first heard about G. K. C. when he was a student at Yale in 1909: "I think it was Professor Chauncey B. Tinker who recommended him in class that year, and I seem to remember that William Lyon Phelps was also a Chesterton enthusiast at that early period. The book that helped and influenced me most was 'The Everlasting Man.' I liked it so well that I bought three copies, intending to lend them to as many people as possible, for I thought the whole world should drink at that fountain of wisdom. I soon discovered, however, that some people loved the book and others hated it just as feverently. This was to be expected, perhaps, about anything so profoundly Christian in its perceptions. In fact, I began to entertain an almost superstitious notion that the book had a practical value apart from literary considerations, in what St. Ignatius, following St. John, called the Discernment of Spirits. The various agnostics and pagans to whom I lent the book usually kept it a long while, and finally returned it saying apologetically that they had never found time to read it, though I knew that every one of them had read several other books in the interim. Finally the three volumes

118

disappeared completely from my life. It was partly my fault, for I have a bad habit of lending books, and forgetting to whom: and as the number of people who have to be reminded to return books is apparently very large, I have lost the best part of my library in consequence: for it is usually the book that one is enthusiastic about that one lends. But I can't help thinking the Devil must have had a particular grudge against so true and so powerful a book, and has continued to hide all three of my volumes on the most obscure shelves of as many sons of Belial. Still, as good comes out of evil in the long run, it may be that the sons of these benighted individuals may inadvertently come upon them on rainy days, and in their innocence read and be enlightened.

"In my biography of Philip the Second, I have had to differ with Chesterton's interpretations of that most misunderstood gentleman. But when G. K wrote his glorious 'Lepanto,' he was still partly deceived by the tradition that had so long dominated English letters, so far as Spain was concerned. It is the only mistake of importance I have ever noted in the work of that phenomenal man."

Hamlin Garland met him at the Savage Club in London, and several times in America: "As a matter of fact, I introduced him when he made his first address in New York City. I enjoyed his mystery stories much better than some of his more pretentious work. From my point of view he worked the paradoxes altogether too hard. He was a very singular and interesting character."

Waldo Frank remembers that when he was "in college and out of it, the essays of G. K. C. stimulated me, indeed. His critique of modern society, his destruction of its complacencies, his suggestive references to other values now absent, meant a good deal to me."

Myles Connolly feels that Chesterton "will not, try as I will, come under the head of remembrance. He seems vividly contemporary, vitally alive. It's a worn-out form of tribute, I know, but there's none greater and I will say it: he lives. The stuff of immortality was so strong in him that beside his memory as the world calls it, it is we who are dead.

"Napoleon said that no man became a writer unless he were a defeatist. When life was too tall and strong for a man, he quit, and in his pen he found corroboration and consolation. That is not, we are aware, altogether so. Although it is true most men who write are running away. But with Chester-

ton writing was not running away; it
was running to—running to reality, to
truth. Writing was life with him: it
was his breathing, his talk, his laughter, his self. It might be said that
those who don't like Chesterton don't
like the truth. It might ever more accurately be said that those who don't
like Chesterton, don't like life. That
superabundance of his, that hugeness
of his, is too much for them. They
crawl; he dances (albeit like the mountains of Scripture). They pick-peck;
he waves that tremendous sword. They
count those corroded little pennies; he
empties that fabulous purse of his on
the world. He was an extravagant man;
extravagant of his riches, his light, his
life. It is this shining extravagance
that blinds the crawlers and pick-peckers
and misers. It is a glory too much for
them. A few words of 'Thoreau' are, I
think, to the point. 'I fear,' writes the
Concord ascetic, 'lest my expression
may not be **extra-vagrant** enough, may
not wander far enough beyond the narrow limits of my daily experience, so as
to be adequate to the truth of which I
have been convinced . . . I desire to
speak somewhere without bounds; like
a man in a waking moment to men in
their waking moments; for I am convinced I cannot exaggerate enough even
to lay the foundation of a true expres-

121

sion  Who that has heard a strain of music feared then lest he should speak extravagantly any more forever?'

"To Chesterton such words as 'tremendous' and 'splendid' and 'enormous' and 'shattering' were of common use. (In fact, it was he who made such words popular.) These words came naturally to him because (and he would be the last to admit it) he himself lived these words; such words only could express his vitality and signifcance. He was a giant. There is no other way of saying it. Except, perhaps, to say he still is."

James Branch Cabell "enjoyed all the work of Chesterton's early and middle period. I admit that of his publications during, let us say vaguely, more recent years, I prefer to say nothing, out of loyalty to a person that has given me a vast amount of pleasure. I write this after verifying the fact that his earlier books when I re-read them, can still do this."

"Indeed I am a warm admirer of Chesterton," affirms Rabbi Stephen S. Wise. "Apart from his delightful wit and his genius in many directions, he was a great religionist. He as a Catholic, I as a Jew, could see eye to eye with each other, and he might have added, 'particularly seeing that you are cross-eyed;' but I deeply respected him.

122

When Hitlerism came, he was one of the first to speak out with all the directness and frankness of a great and unabashed spirit."

Dr. Alexis Carrel well remembers that "Heretics" was the first Chesterton book that he read almost a quarter of a century ago,

"The extreme clarity and brilliance of his style impressed me greatly. The train of his thought appeared to me as strong, flexible, and shining as a steel blade, and as merciless."

# CHAPTER ELEVEN†

## THE AUTHOR VISITS TOP MEADOW

In a delightful villa, called Top Meadow, in Beaconsfield, a small town of Buckinghamshire, about forty minutes on the train from London, lives, and has lived for some ten years, Gilbert Keith Chesterton with his charming wife. Chesterton, a huge man, possesses the frankness and enthusiasm of a boy, with unkept curly blond hair, blue eyes, shaggy reddish brown moustache, an exceedingly pleasant and attractive smile, wearing clothes in a somewhat careless and negligent manner. Although clear and resonant, his voice is not as powerful as one would be led to expect for a man of his size. He possesses the little mannerism of twirling the ends of his moustache every now and then. He would make a joke with true Twainian seriousness upon his face, but unlike the great American such feigned seriousness becomes too much for him, and he bursts

† This entire chapter was read, corrected, and approved in its present shape, by Chesterton himself a short time before his death.

out in peals of Gargantuan laughter that often renders him speechless for a few seconds. At other times the idea of something funny will cause him to laugh most heartily before he has had a chance to express it in words.

In a little hallway, Chesterton introduced me to his wife, and then led the way into the living room, a tremendous chamber fully a hundred feet long, low-ceilinged and surrounded on all sides by shelves bulging and overflowing with books of every description, a massive fire-place built of large stones that must have come from the bed of a near-by brook, and a number of what proved to be exceedingly comfortable chairs grouped around the empty fire-place; for it was midsummer.

As we sat down before the fire-place, Chesterton said he was vastly amused over a delegation from America that had called on him the day before.

"They were making a tour of Europe for the express purpose of unearthing everything they could about Browning. They called on me because I have once written a book on the poet. It was a grave mistake on their part to think that because a man has written a book on a particular subject in the dim and distant past, he therefore knows everything about that subject. At the time of writing the book, I probably was a little more up on Robert Browning than the average person, but all my superior knowledge has slipped from me long ago."

The question of modern youth came up for discussion.

"Young people today have the idea that old timers are landmarks. I hope I do not fill as much space as Saint Paul's, but at least I am a Victorian ruin dating from the year 1874. The last time I was in New York I noticed that the landscape was always changing. When a baby is born he just has time to look at the skyscrapers a week or so before they are pulled down. Pulling down New York seems to be the local industry. A baby goes out in his perambulator and his home is pulled down before he gets back."

"What do you think of the young people today, Mr. Chesterton?"

"Well," he replied, "their chief trouble is they don't want to admit that old people really do know the modern movement because we are able to compare it with movements of the past. But the young people know nothing else but the present. The result is that they do not give modern conditions much thought. For instance, if we had moving sidewalks today, the young people would take it for granted, the old ones alone

126

could compare them with the stationary sidewalks."

"Do you think that much change has taken place in the last fifty years," I asked.

"We cannot grasp the tremendous change that has taken place since 1874, my birth year. Your country used not to pay much attention to culture. When Matthew Arnold began his lecture series in America, he was worried about what the American papers would say of him for his criticism of certain phases of American culture which he had handled rather severely, but was relieved to find that the papers had large headlines reading,

" 'Matthew Arnold has side whiskers.' But today you have a very high regard for culture in your country."

"What literary people did you meet in America, Mr. Chesterton?"

"Among others I met Robert Cortes Holliday, and Sinclair Lewis," he replied. "I found Lewis a pleasant fellow. He was anxious to learn about the conditions in England. That man, I think, has considerable genius. I met 'A. E.' George Russell, also when I was at Yale. He was completely wrapped up in giving his lectures on agriculture to you Americans."

"What does he think of our country?"

"He has a semi-humorous, rather critical, attitude towards you. He won't write anything much in praise or anything particularly hostile."†

"What American cities especially appealed to you?"

"Baltimore I found exceedingly charming," answered Chesterton. "There is a quaint atmosphere about the place that is hard to describe. Saint Louis I also liked, a most pleasant cultured city."

"I once heard you lecture in Saint Louis, Mr. Chesterton," I remarked, "and I agree with what you said about the underdog:

" 'When the very poor man gets angry and 'bites,' everyone, even the social workers, treat him as though he were a mad dog. Has he not the right to get deliberately angry, the same as anybody else? Once I debated with Clarence Darrow, and when I talked to him after the lecture, he seemed to have sympathy for the poor man, the underdog, who was goaded on to do things, by saying that he was mad. Why cannot people give the underdog credit for biting when he wants to, instead of contending that he is just the same as a mad dog on a rampage?' "

---

† This prophesy of Chesterton's proved to be correct.

When Galsworthy became the topic of conversation, Chesterton remarked,

"Galsworthy always reminds me of the solicitor of an old English family. I cannot altogether feel that he reflects modern England. He lays too much stress upon a college education. He believes that a man not blessed with a college education might at any time murder his mother. Galsworthy also lacks the sweet balance of humor, only a rather limited amount of humor breathes forth from his works. Like Darrow he, too, holds to the belief that the underdog is always mad if he causes the slightest trouble.

"Again Galsworthy never seems to write with set purpose, while I am one of those people who believe that you've got to be dominated by your moral slant. I'm no 'art-for-art's-sake' man. I am quite incapable of talking or writing about Dutch gardens or the game of chess, but if I did, I have no doubt that what I say or write about them would be colored by my view of the cosmos."

When the question of pessimism came up, I mentioned that the week before I had had the pleasure of dining with A. E. Housman at Cambridge †

---

† See "An Evening with A. E. Housman," by Cyril Clemens, 1937.

129

who facetiously told me that he was often compared to Hardy because both their names began with an "H".

"That is all the basis critics often have for forming comparisons," replied Chesterton with a smile, "but in this case there is a measure of truth in the comparison. Both undoubtedly have a certain amount of pessimism. Poet Housman's, however, has the tang of the fresh air about it, whereas Hardy's seems somewhat unpleasant."

And to illustrate his point, Chesterton quoted from "A Shropshire Lad,"

"Oh many a peer of England brews
Livelier liquor than the Muse,
And malt does more than Milton can
To justify God's ways to man.
Ale, man, ale's the stuff to drink
For fellows whom it hurts to think:
Look into the pewter pot
To see the world as the world's not."

A little later we went to the small dining room which was a few steps higher than, and was separated by a heavy silk curtain from, the living room. At a massive oaken table we sat down to a delicious tea.

When I asked Mrs. Chesterton what was the national dish of England, she promptly replied,

"Roast beef and Yorkshire pudding, undoubtedly."

"Fried eggs and bacon is my favorite dish," spoke up Chesterton.

I then asked the author what would be his choice if he had to go on a desert island and could take but one book along.

"It would depend upon the circumstances," he replied. "If I were a politician who wanted to impress his constituents, I would take Plato or Aristotle. But the real test would be with people who had no chance to show off before their friends or their constituents. In that case I feel certain that everyone would take Thomas' 'Guide to Practical Shipbuilding' so that they could get away from the island as quickly as possible. And then if they should be allowed to take a second book it would be the most exciting detective story within reach. But if I could only take one book to a desert isle and was not in a particular hurry to get off, I would without the slightest hesitation put 'Pickwick Papers' in my handbag."

The talk switched to the Russian situation. Chesterton thinks that Lenin was of the mad Russian type, just such a type as Tolstoy,

"But Trotsky is at once both more commercial and cunning; he is the typical Russian or German Jew."

The Chestertons own a pert little Scotch terrier named Quoodle. "I named him Quoodle," explained Chesterton, "after the hero of one of my early, but alas forgotten, novels, in the hope that unwary visitors like you would ask about the origin of the name and I would have a good excuse to talk about my novel! But when only the family is present we shorten the name to Quo: a handy name and one that can be yelled to the top of the lungs."

Among the other delectable viands that Mrs. Chesterton's bounty provided were some cakes made out of the white of eggs, that caused me to say,

"These cakes put me in mind of some period of English Literature."

"They remind me, rather," responded Chesterton with a hearty laugh, "of icebergs and I wish that I was sitting on a large one just now. (It was an extremely hot August afternoon.) But if we must compare them to some period of English literature they remind me of the rococo period, the age of Horace Walpole, in particular of some of the decorations of his home 'Strawberry Hill'."

Tea over, Chesterton suggested going to see his garden. After putting on an enormous sombrero, and taking in his hand something like a small axe, but which proved to be a walking stick which his Polish friend, Roman Dyboski, had given him, he led the way

132

through a French window out into a
tidy little garden. We sat on camp
chairs in a pleasant spot. Chesterton's
one seemed somewhat frail, shaking a
little, and to make matters worse, the
cat Stanley Baldwin came along and
fell sound asleep right under his master's chair! If anything had happened
to the chair, Baldwin would have
awakened in cat heaven!

The conversation turned on the rather whimsical subject of chairs.

"H. G. Wells in one of his books," remarked Chesterton, "has written several pages on the subject of chairs.
Some non-materialists might very well
contend there is no such a thing as a
chair. They would argue that since
there are all kinds and varieties of
chairs, when you use the word 'chair'
you cannot have any particular one in
mind: therefore the word is only ab-
stract and hence has no equivalent in
actuality!"

When I wondered if anything had
ever been written on the subject of
shoes, Chesterton answered that his
friend Hilaire Belloc had done an exceedingly entertaining essay on the
subject, "Belloc makes the point that
the kind of shoes a man wears and how
he keeps them, is a better indication of
his character, than any other piece of
apparel."

133

Chesterton told of a literary club
which had lately given a fancy dressed
ball for its members, and that he went
as Doctor Samuel Johnson. When I
asked who Mrs. Chesterton went as, he
replied with a merry twinkle in his eye,

"My wife went dressed as one of the
characters in a novel that I am going
to write in the near future! You see
that I devise ways and means to ad-
vertise both my old novels and my new
ones!"

The subject of Rome and Mussolini
came up, and when I expressed admiration for "The Resurrection of Rome,"
he snapped,

"I think it was a pretty bad book."

At my disagreement, a look of mild
surprise appeared on Chesterton's face,

"Well," explained he, "it was written
just after a stay in Rome, and I think
that I made the fatal mistake of reading the book too soon after it was written. That should never be done by any
author. The longer after the writing
that I wait to read one of my books, the
better it seems."

When I mentioned that Mussolini had
told me how much he had enjoyed reading "The Man Who Was Thursday,"
and had found it exceedingly funny,
Chesterton answered,

"Does anyone find my books funny?
It pleases me to hear that, for at times

I fear that my humorous works are taken seriously and my serious ones humorously. I also had an audience with Mussolini. He did not act in a high and mighty manner at all, but showed a genuine interest in England and asked me numerous questions about the country. He was indeed a jolly card."

"In what language did you carry on your conversation," I asked.

"We spoke in French," replied Chesterton, "and when leaving I said, 'I hope you excused my poor French, Your Excellency.' To which Mussolini answered, 'That's all right; you speak French about as well as I speak English'."

After a moment's pause Chesterton reflected, "I don't suppose that was much of a compliment for my French, because at that time Mussolini knew practically no English."

"When do you do most of your writing, Mr. Chesterton?"

"Whenever I get a chance, I do not care much for the typewriter and I find pen or pencil much too tedious, for I am a rather slow writer. At present I do a considerable amount of dictating. I can compose just as readily this way."

One of the last questions I asked my host was his opinion of Mark Twain,

"I have always admired the genius of Mark Twain which may truly be

135

called gigantic. Mark Twain dealt so
much with the gigantic exaggeration
of imagination; the skyscrapers of literature. He was the greatest master of
the tall story who has ever lived and
was also, what is more important, a
thoroughly sincere man."

As the cab to take me to my London
train was announced, Chesterton grac-
iously inscribed his "History of England" in the following fashion,

"Greetings to the Mark Twain Society
from an Innocent at Home
G. K. Chesterton
Known as the Unjumping Frog of
Bucks County."

and Mrs. Chesterton added,
"And from Frances Chesterton
Wife of the Innocent."

# CHAPTER TWELVE

## FATHER BROWN.

Once in telling his creator what delight Father Brown had given him, the author asked if the spiritual detective was a real person.

"Indeed he is," answered Chesterton. "His name is Father John O'Connor and he lives in Bradford, Yorkshire."

" 'Trent's Last Case' had recently appeared," Father O'Connor himself writes the author, "and Chesterton full of admiration for E. C. Bentley, was humbly envious, longing to add to the small (as it was then) crop of detective stories. He also was bitten with costume drama and would without provocation 'lurk' by the jamb of a doorway with cloak-and-sword (he had a sword-stick) as it were in wait for the Duke of Guise. He had a column the next week in 'The Daily News,' relating how the forest-keepers of Ilkley apprehended him for making passes at the local trees, but released him on learning that he was a guest of a Justice of the Peace.

"Many a glorious day we had together under that hospitable roof of Francis Steinthal and his ever gracious wife. Chesterton himself tells how two young men that first evening, after I had gone home, wondered how a sheltered existence like mine could ever take part in the rude, naughty world as it stood, and how this gave the first push off to the Father Brown series. Disguise is mingled with description— I did carry a specially large and cheap umbrella—had quite a habit of brown-paper parcels—and the episode of the sapphire cross—(in America, a diamond cross, of course) has this relation to sordid fact, that I was still vain in having bought five sapphires for five shillings in an obscure pawnshop in Bradford. Many years later, in Bradford again, some duffer introduced me as Father Brown to two international crooks who were playing themselves into the book-trade, and they both disappeared, leaving no trace, within twenty-four hours!"

Father O'Connor never forgot the day that he spent with the two Chesterton brothers at St. John's, Ilkley, and has often wondered since if anyone ever had a better chance to observe their mental difference and their deep attachment at such close quarters as he did that day. Cecil was a Church of England Conservative Fabian Socialist,

Gilbert was almost an official Liberal, and at that time writing for "The Daily News." Cecil had already, in "'The Fabian Review," bettered daylight through the Liberal Party in many a large hole. This can be seen in his "Gladstonian Ghosts." From lunch till tea and from tea till dinner, Cecil stood his ground, and Gilbert must have walked many miles around the large dining table trying to reply to his brother's arguments.

Chesterton gave the author his own version of how he first conceived the idea for the famous character,

"While at tea with Father O'Connor the conversation turned to philosophical and moral channels, and I mentioned with considerable timidity, a certain rather sordid question of vice and crime, which I intended to discuss in a future essay. I was vastly astonished to find that the priest not only had a thorough working knowledge of the subject but was able to furnish me with further facts of an almost sensational nature.

"Some days later Father O'Connor and I took dinner with two Cambridge undergraduates. When the priest left the room, the young men remarked on what a thoroughly charming and cultivated person he was despite the fact that in his cloistered existence he knew so little of the world. One of them remarked, 'It's a very beautiful thing to be innocent and ignorant, but I think it's a much finer thing not to be afraid of knowledge.'

"The complete and crushing irony of the remark so touched my imagination that there was born in my mind the idea of a priest who should appear to know nothing, but as a matter of fact, know more about crime than the criminals themselves. The point of him (Father Brown) was to appear pointless; and one might say that his conspicuous quality was in NOT being conspicuous. I have always thought that the most appropriate compliment ever paid my famous detective priest came from the lips of a charming Catholic lady who remarked, 'I am very fond of that 'officious little loafer'.' "

The prototype of one of the Father Brown characters, Hesketh Pearson, writes the author,

"I greatly enjoyed the Father Brown stories, and remember his telling me that he had described me in one of them, though I cannot remember which. My last meeting with him was not altogether a pleasant one because he started it by asking,

" 'Why, are you not a Catholic? All the best writers of today are Catholics

140

and you are much too clever to be anything else!'

"I was forced to explain my view of God, which was not his, and this disagreement cast a slight shade over the subsequent conversation—though I am sure he was much too kindly a soul to let it affect his feelings towards me, which were always most cordial. He was extremely generous to me at two crucial moments in my life, and I shall always remember h'm with gratitude, admiration and affection."

Rafael Sabatini's first acquaintance with Chesterton's work "was made through Father Brown, and I don't know that I cared more for any of his creations. He was, we all know, one of three contemporaries to whom allusion was commonly made by their triple initials: G. K. C. in his case. The other two, G. B. S. (George Bernard Shaw and Clement K. Shorter). One day that perverse genius, T. W. H. Crossland (of whom little may have been known in the States) was in my study chatting with me in his usual disgruntled fashion. The conversation turned on Shorter. Whilst he talked he scribbled on a British Museum reading room ticket, which he left carelessly on my table. After he had gone I looked at the ticket and found on it scribbled the following quatrain, which has remained hitherto unpublished,

'G. K. S.
G. K. C.
G. B. S.
N. B. G.' "

G. B. Stern has "received intense pleasure from a good deal of G. K. C. One of my most treasured books is a first edition of 'The Napoleon of Notting Hill' which excited me wildly when I first read it, some time in my teens. I was born in Holland Park, and used to be sent as a child for daily walks all over Campden Hill and up and down through 'Napoleon' kingdom, so that it had a strong local interest as well as its romantic appeal. I think, therefore, this remains the favorite of his works, together with 'Lepanto,' 'The Secret People,' and two or three of the other poems; but I also greatly enjoy and have re-read several times the Father Brown stories and 'The Flying Inn.' Also I was present at the very first performance in London of the play, 'Magic,' which seemed to me even then inspired with those queer colored bursts of truth which were so peculiarly Chesterton."

The late Mr. S. S. Van Dine, author of "The 'Canary' Murder Case" and "The Philo Vance Murder Case," wrote the author, "I am very glad to be included

as one of America's admirers of G. K.
C.'s Father Brown series. Father Brown
has long been a favorite with me."

And Mary Roberts Rinehart, "Of
course I was a great admirer of the
Father Brown stories, and was naturally pleased that Mr. Chesterton liked
my own work. In a way we formed a
sort of mutual admiration society."

"Chesterton and I wrote a detective
story together," recalls Sir Max Pemberton. "I opened the mystery—he
closed it, most ably, of course. I can't
remember what it was about, but I am
sure he brought the villain to justice.

"He was a truly great figure—a
worthy successor to the immortal Doctor Johnson. Both had rare gifts, of
literature and Faith."

# CHAPTER THIRTEEN

## SOME APPRAISALS.

"Chesterton was one of the great and dynamic forces during the time he lived," declares Ralph Adams Cram. "I 'fell for him' many years ago when almost by accident I found and read 'The Napoleon of Notting Hill.' That settled the case for me, and after that I was, so to speak, his intellectual and spiritual slave. Of all his books it seems to me this, together with 'The Man Who Was Thursday,' 'The Bell and the Cross,' 'The Flying Inn' and 'The Victorian Age of English Literature' are those for which I care most. This may seem a curious selection, but in most of these he makes his points through indirection, and in some ways this seems to me a more powerful method of conveying his ideas and inspiring the public than the more explicit works, the object of which is very obvious. This is not to disparage anything he ever did —except, perhaps, the Father Brown Mystery stories, which seem to me rather unworthy of him, though even these serve to show the immense

144

breadth of his interest, his knowledge, and his literary ability."

The late W. B. Yeats wrote the author that he found Chesterton "a kindly and generous man of whom I constantly heard from friends, but as far as I can recollect I only met him socially twice, once at a Club dinner and once for tea at a country house. So much of my life has always been spent in Ireland that I know comparatively little of the English celebrities. I don't want to write about his works: I have read very little of it, and to write even of that little would open up great questions I don't want to come to any decision about in my present ignorance (which is likely to endure)."

In his "Autobiography," Chesterton states that he had some talk about poetry and property with Yeats at the Dublin Art Club, "a most exhilarating evening." Yeats asked Chesterton to debate at the Abbey Theatre, defending property on its more purely political side, against an able leader of Liberty Hall, the famous stronghold of Labor politics in Dublin, Robert Johnson, who was exceedingly popular with the proletarian Irish.

"That passage from G. K. C.'s 'Autobiography' is correct so far as I can remember," wrote Yeats in a second letter. "It was a time when the English

145

Government was stopping discussion and we kept discussion open at the Abbey Theatre when it had stopped elsewhere, by getting people to speak on the conservative side and letting debate develop as it like afterwards. Johnson who replied to Chesterton was at that time the most important Irish labour leader: he is still very important. He was in the Irish Senate for some years, Bernard Shaw lectured either the week after or the week before Chesterton. Both men were brilliant, Chesterton taking the line that the possession of small properties was ensential to liberty, Johnson putting the Trades Union point of view that it was more important for the workman to spend his money on his children than to save it."

Cuthbert Wright's only personal connection with Chesterton was to have been mentioned in one of his last books, "The Well and the Shadows": "Some year ago I had published a review of G. K. C.'s 'Catholic Church and Conversion,' in which I drew attention to what I considered a stylistic defect, his mania for alliteration. He seems to have remembered it during the intervening years, and doing me the honor to couple my name with that of Mr. T. S. Eliot wrote as follows,

" 'It must be a terrible strain on the

presence of mind to be always ready with a synonym. I can imagine Mr. T. S. Eliot just stopping himself in time and saying, 'Waste not, require not.' I like to think of Mr. Cuthbert Wright having the self-control to cry, 'Time and fluctuation wait for no man.' I can imagine his delicate accent when speaking of a pig in a receptacle or of bats in the campanile."

Professor Roman Dyboski of Krakow, Poland, was first drawn to Chesterton when he read some articles in the "Illustrated London News," and some passages from his historical poem, "The Ballad of the White Horse." The professor suggested his advanced students making a special study on the author, and the result was two Polish books on G. K. C. Soon translations of Chesterton's works became fairly numerous in Poland. His play "Magic" had several successful runs on Polish stages, and the Polish Radio popularized "The Man Who Was Thursday" in a dramatic version.

Shortly after his visit to Poland early in 1927, Chesterton sent Dr. Dyboski an introduction to a collective volume of studies by Polish scholars written to commemorate the Seventh Hundred Anniversary of the death of St. Francis of Assisi, and the services of the Franciscans to civilization.

147

On July 7, 1927, Chesterton spoke
on Poland at the Essex Hall in the
Strand. Crowds of his admirers were
present; the late Cardinal Bourne himself appeared on the platform; the
Polish Ambassador took the chair;
Hilaire Belloc moved the vote of thanks
which was seconded by Dyboski. The
first part of the address struck all present as the most illuminating English
opinion that had ever been expressed
on Poland,

"I am to speak on Poland, a country
very unfamiliar to the average English
person. In order to facilitate approach
to the subject, let me begin by saying
that Poland is Poland. This is the
kind of statement which, when I make
it, is of course called a paradox (Laughter). Yet what I wish to express is
something quite plain and simple.
Those of you who have studied medieval history, may remember the ancient kingdom of Bohemia—situated, according to Shakespeare, by the sea-side
—now you hear much of Czechoslo-
vakia, unknown to you before. Again,
those of you who are old enough to remember the World War, will recall the
fervent admiration which we all felt for
the heroism of the Servian nation: now
we often hear the name of Yugoslavia,
which we never heard in those days.
As for Poland, she is now known by the

148

same name which she bore through centuries, when she was a great power in Europe, and by which our fathers knew her to exist in those days when she had disappeared from the map, yet continued to live as a nation and to struggle for freedom. That is why I begin by saying that Poland is Poland, and submit that as a fundamental fact for you to consider before we go further."

It is difficult to imagine more eloquent and emphatic words of recognition for the continuity of Poland's national tradition through eight centuries of recorded independent existence, through a century and more of division and captivity, and into the dawn of reunion and regained liberty. Chesterton, who in these words as well as in various poems and essays, always acknowledged in Poland one of the corner-stones of the historical structure of European civilization, remained a faithful friend of Poland to his death.

"Grey Beards at Play," a book of poems in the Mark Twain tradition with G. K.'s own illustrations, first impressed the philosopher L. E. Gilson. But the book which remains with him as the most stimulating is "Orthodoxy," "When it came out I hailed it as the best piece of apologetic the century had produced. In a sense all his later works

149

are a variation on the same theme. I was interested in the biography of the conversion of a well known American financial expert whose conversion was brought about by reading in succession Chesterton's 'O r t h o d o x y ,' Fulton Sheen's 'God and the Intelligence,' and Karl Adams' 'Spirit of Catholicism.' I don't wonder they would convert the Devil if he had a sense of humor, and open mind, and could pray for grace!"

Mr. Gilson believes that Chesterton will not really be fully appreciated before a century or two. The book of his which he likes best is "St. Thomas Aquinas:" "I consider is as being without possible comparison the best book ever written on St. Thomas. Nothing short of genius can account for such an achievement. Everybody will no doubt admit that it is a 'clever' book, but the few readers who have spent twenty or thirty years in studying St. Thomas Aquinas, and who, perhaps, have themselves published two or three volumes on the subject, cannot fail to perceive that the so-called 'wit' of Chesterton has put their scholarship to shame. He has guessed all that which we had tried to demonstrate, and he has said all that which they were more or less clumsily attempting to express in academic formulas. Chesterton was one of the deepest thinkers who ever existed; he was

150

deep because he was right; and he could not help being right; but he could not either help being modest and charitable, so he left it to those who could understand him to know that he was right, and deep; to the others, he apologized for being right, and he made up for being deep by being witty. That is all they can see of him."

Eileen Duggan gives the opinion of a New Zealander,

"One of the innumerable society diarists who writes for a hobby recorded an anecdote that illustrates Chesterton's complete absorption in a subject. He had been given, rather foolishly, a little gold period chair, and as he made his points, it slowly crashed beneath him. He rose just in time and sinking into another chair that someone put behind him, began at the word he had last spoken. It was evident to all that he had barely noticed the incident rather than that he had decided to ignore it.

"A New Zealander who heard him lecture relates that his appearance after a long delay caused the Chairman to express relief that he had not been knocked down by a tramcar. G. K. C. rose calmly and thanked him for his solicitude, 'but,' said he, 'Mr. Chairman, had I met a tramcar it would have been

151

a great and, if, I may say so, an equal encounter.' "

"His journalistic training," continues Miss Duggan, "had taught him simplification and the author of those penetrating studies on Dickens and Browning would put his points on Distributism so that they could be understood by the man in the street. A sacrifice seemed worthless to Chesterton, unless it were voluntary and not State-imposed; in Distributism, then, he saw the solution of the world's problems, the answer for soul and for body of its ills.

"It has been charged that he was the enemy of Jewry, but his hand was against only a small and powerful Oligarchy within it which, he claimed, harmed the poor Jew of the ghetto more than the Gentile and, commenting on the anti-Jewish excesses which have outraged the world, he said that he had now to defend the Jews against Hitler. It will be remembered that he struck at all internal abuses and certain lines of his were arrowheads in the national flesh. These for instance, on postwar corruption drew blood,

" 'Oh, they that fought for England,
Following a fallen star,
Alas, alas for England!
They have their graves afar.

152

But they that rule in England
In stately conclave met,
Alas, alas for England!
They have no graves as yet.'

"He was a Little Englander; partly,
one suspects, as a reaction from Kip-
lingism: but in an age of peace he was
a defender of just wars. He inveighed
against those who blamed the older
generation in 1914 when they decided
that war was the only honorable solution and later he said that a universal
peace, founded on a universal panic,
raised the point as to whether the supreme moral state will be found when
everybody is too frightened to fight;
and dying, but undefeated, he repeated
as a creed, 'Monarchy, aristocracy, democracy — responsible forms of rule—
have collapsed under plutocracy, which
is irresponsible rule. And this has
come upon us because we departed from
the old morality in three essential
points. First, we supported notions
against known, old customs; secondly,
we made the state top-heavy with a
new and secretive tyranny of will; and
third, we forgot that there is no faith
in freedom without faith in free-will.
Materialism brings with it a servile
fatalism—because nothing, as Dante
said, else than 'the generosity of God
could give to man after all ordinary,

orderly gifts, the noblest of all things which is——liberty.' "

Chesterton examined and scrutinized the conscience of England as he did his own, but only a fool would deny that from York to Cornwall he loved his country with a Little Englander's passion!

# CHAPTER FOURTEEN

## THE POET

Not a few of his readers feel that Chesterton's chief bid to fame is his poetry. Alfred Noyes, for instance, writes the author,

"Chesterton led one of the most original lives of his day in Europe. It is well to remember this when it is suggested that men who avail themselves of the rich experiences of the centuries are merely echoes of the past. The true originality does not consist in inventing ideas that have no relation to truth and no roots in reality, but in the discovery and unveiling of something that has always been there, though we may hitherto have lacked the eyes to see it, or the power to express and interpret it. Chesterton had an expert gift for making one see things in all their original miscellaneousness, as things that really **are,** and yet—**cannot** be, or give any rational account of themselves. Many years ago in a poem on the death of Francis Thompson, I wrote of the overwhelming mystery that there should be a single grain of

155

dust in existence, the sheer impossibility of it on any rational ground, and how the smallest atom defied exploration and ultimately asserted a super-rational origin.

"'I am . . . yet cannot be, . . .!

"Chesterton tosses out his thoughts in a glorious liberality; but I am proud to think that this line unconsciously found its way into two of Chesterton's poems afterwards — 'The House of Christmas,' where he speaks of 'the things that cannot be, and that are,' and the splendid lyric 'Second Childhood,' where he says,

"'And stones still shine along the roads
That are and cannot be!'

"Like most men of genius he kept his own immortal childhood all his life; and it was in the matrix of it, the vision that 'saw' as a manifestation of something 'supernatural,' 'something that ultimately defied reason, not because it was merely difficult to understand, but because it rested on an eternal and absolute mystery (above and beyond the range of secondary causes) it was in this wonder at the abiding in the terrestrial that he made me feel the power of his faith,

" 'When all my days are ending
    And I have no songs to sing
I think I shall not be too old
    To stare at everything,
As I stared once at a nursery door
    Or a tall tree and a swing—

Strange crawling carpets of the grass
    Wide windows of the sky—'

"One of the greatest of all his poems
is the sonnet entitled 'The Convert,' in
which he describes how, after he had
'bowed his head,' he came out where
the old world shone white, and heard
'myriads of tongues like autumn leaves,'
'not so loveable,' but 'strange and light,'
in their whispering assumption that,
among the old riddles and new creeds,
he must now be taken as belonging to
a dead past.  He sees them singing—
not harshly—'but softly as men smile
about the dead.'  And then comes this
magnificent and soul-stirring challenge
from the 'dead man',

" 'The sages have a hundred maps to
        give
    That trace their crawling cosmos like
        a tree.
    They rattle reason out through many
        a sieve
    That holds the soil, but lets the gold
        go free;

And all these things are less than
  dust to me
Because my name is Lazarus, and I
  live!' "

Francis B. Thornton, the authority
on Gerald Manley Hopkins, first knew
Chesterton through his drinking songs,
"An admirable introduction; they were
so much more than their title signifies,
and they transported me to the happy
age which preceded the Malvolios and
their hatred of cakes and ale. To me
Chesterton will always be the poet. He
not only saw what other men looked at,
he saw **through** as well, and it was this
faculty which gave an angelic quality
to his humor. He was like a bull in a
china shop, but it was a papal bull enun-
ciating principles in the midst of a
wreck of fragile half-truth."

Mr. J. Corson Miller "was introduced
to the poetry of Chesterton by Mr.
William Rose Benet who dilated on the
vigor and splendor of 'The Ballad of the
White Horse.' I read that magnificent
work, and thereafter read all the verse
that G. K. C. produced. I am a great
admirer of his poetical work. I admire
his flexible sonnets, with their vast
sweep of thought, and radiant vision.
His various lyrics, love, nature, and religious lyrics, are all excellent; his religious poetry is sublime. His well

known lyric, 'The Donkey,' with its superb last two lines, or couplet, is unforgettable. His 'Queen of the Seven Swords'—his second last, if not his last, published volume of verse, bears in my humble opinion, the breadth and fire of eternal life. His was, indeed, a great spirit: no toadying, or cavilling; no smirking or masking, but strong and free, with the strength of the clean West wind, he put his thoughts and opinions and visions in books and papers, and let the seeds of his ideas fall where they would, with results be what they might. His many-sided genius is well known: political and social economist; poet, historian, novelist, short-story writer, artist and cartoonist, playwright—hardly any field in art and literature can be mentioned—without his having touched it in some manner and left his mark, too."

Prof. Joseph J. Reilly holds that Chesterton will be best remembered for his poetry,

"The initial book I read was 'Varied Types.' My first reaction was one of delight in Chesterton's brilliance, my second a realization that his views were colored so decidedly by his personality that one could not hope to get a genuinely objective appraisal from him. This has always seemed to me an element of strength and of weakness and

159

ever since I have turned to Chesterton's criticism most largely for the unusual flashes of insight which he shows than for any completely balanced judgment. In one sense he is like a delicious dessert: it is not the main part of a dinner but no dinner would be satisfying without it.

"My next acquaintance was with his 'Orthodoxy' which I found full of wisdom, insight, and inspiration. As I went on, I sometimes grew a little weary of his paradoxes but changed my mind when I happened one day upon his statement that to him parodox was 'truth standing on its head.'

"After reading his volume of poems through several times and thinking him over for many months preparatory to writing an article on Chesterton as poet, I came to the conclusion to which I still cling that Chesterton's best claim to the attention of our great-grandchildren will be based on his poetry."

John Gould Fletcher considers "Lepanto" is Chesterton's finest poem, "next to that superb 'Ballad of the White Horse'—too long for most people, I fancy, but absolutely characteristic of his great, generous, simple, and manly nature.

"I did not learn to like his poetry because of a parent or teacher. From my earliest years I have always read all

160

the poets I could lay my hands on; and
in later years, I have continued the
practice. I read 'Lepanto' and the
'Ballad' some time back in 1912 as I
recall, during my early years in London
—read them and liked them. As regards the American poets, I should say
that it was particularly marked in the
case of Vachel Lindsay."

"I am on record," declares Clement
Wood, "that he is the greatest poet of
his generation. I well remember when
'Lepanto' was recited to Vachel Lindsay by Floyd Dell; but Lindsay missed
the rhythm which was ballad measure
—seven beats to the line. Lindsay was
influenced by Chesterton's ballad measure which he re-used in the 'Congo' and
other poems—but as four beats to the
line.

" 'The Ballad of the White Horse' is
the greatest of all modern ballads, possibly the greatest of all ballads,—more
sustainedly memorable, g l o r i o u s
throughout. Many of the shorter pieces,
too, have my warmest admiration."

"The story of my reading 'The Battle
of Lepanto' on the shore of Lake Mich-
igan to Vachel Lindsay is true," declares Floyd Dell. "Note the echo of
'Lepanto' in 'General William Booth,'

"'Dim drums throbbing in the hills
  half heard
Booth enters boldly with his big brass
  drum.'

'Both was the first poem in Vachel's
new style, and followed my chanting
recitation of the poem—which (my way
of reading it) was in turn based on
Yeats' theories of how poetry should
be read. Vachel had an unparalleled
mental possession of the folk tunes (so
to speak) of American speech—camp-
meetings, soap-box, tramp, farmer,
Negro, and so on—but they never broke
through into his own verse until after
he had heard the theory of Yeats and
the poem of Chesterton."

Thomas Caldecot Chubb feels that
Chesterton has been an important influence in the shaping of a brilliant
American poet, "I realize that discuss-
ing influences is dangerous and that
most people like to think of genius as
bursting into the world full grown like
Medusa from the forehead of Jove. But
quite the opposite is usually true and
most men of genius are but the latest—
not the last link—in an unending chain.
They receive, they use, they pass along.
And anyone who will compare 'The
Ballad of the White Horse' with 'The
Drug Shop, or Endymion in Edmons-
toun,' written by Stephen Vincent Benet

162

when he was less than twenty years old, will realize that Benet obtained more than a handful of his poetic implements from Chesterton. This is a paradox in inself, that the gusty panegyrist of the days following the decline of Rome should make an important contribution to so native and so American a voice."

No better way to end this chapter than with what Stephen Vincent Benet writes the author,

"Thank you for sending me your Chapter on Chesterton's poetry which I have read with much interest. I have always greatly admired both 'Lepanto' and the 'Ballad of the White Horse' and I still re-read them."

# CHAPTER FIFTEEN

## CHESTERTON THE MAN

Chesterton possessed one of the most likeable characters of contemporary literary men. There is usually something or other that mars the characters of most, but who would have Chesterton different? Even his faults are beloved: his weight, his tardiness, his absent-mindedness, his slovenly manner of dressing, his sometimes careless way of eating and drinking. In short he can almost be described as Falstaff without his moral grossness.

Chesterton lived for many years in a flat overlooking the beautiful Battersea Park, where Mrs. Lillian Curt would often see him strolling in deep thought. His wife Frances—a dainty little lady, clever and level-headed and most devoted to her husband—would sometimes get anxious when he was long overdue for meals. Then quickly donning her outdoor garments she would anxiously start off to find him, remarking, "I am off to seek my Mighty Atom." The reference being to Marie

164

Corelli's "The Mighty Atom" which had
but recently appeared.

"I knew G. K. C.," writes A. Hamilton Gibbs, "when I was in process of
becoming an undergraduate at Oxford.
Being so grotesquely fat that he
couldn't dress himself he used to appear
in socks at breakfast, eat hugely, and
then go out into the garden with a pad
of paper and a packet of cigarettes. In
the course of a couple of hours there
would be a ring of cigarettes on the
grass around him and when the wind
blew away his pages, he would scream
for help with a series of epigrams
which I am sure found their way into
his later pages. Whenever he went
from the country to London there was
always a little black bag in his hand.
In the bag was a bottle of wine, and in
the station refreshment room he would
order a cup of tea and a wine glass.
Many times I've seen him taking alternate sips of tea and wine between
mouths of a penny bun!"

Whenever he visited Glasgow, Chesterton stayed with Professor Phillimore
who occupied the Greek chair at Glasgow University. Phillimore entertained many literary people in Glasgow,
Hilaire Belloc, Thomas Hardy, Galsworthy, and so forth. Usually disengaged in the mornings, the visitors were
often brought to the Annam Gallery to

be entertained by looking at paintings and etchings. Mr. Annam had the opportunity of making photographic portraits of Chesterton in 1912, when the latter was at his bulkiest. He seemed much interested in his striking appearance and in his likeness to Dr. Johnson. He wore a dark grey highland cloak and a tiny Homburg hat. As he was leaving the studio a small boy stopped and stared at the great man. G. K. noticed the youngster's interest and puffed himself out to his very biggest for his benefit. Nothing was said, of course, but the pose was obvious. In the course of conversation he made various references to his appearance.

Mrs. Hugh C. Riviere remembers Chesterton as a school boy at St. Paul's, a tall slim youth who even then had the feeling of the romance of weapons that runs through so much of his work. He went to stay with Mr. and Mrs. Riviere after his marriage when his wife was ill in bed and unable to see to his packing. The result was that he arrived **with nothing** but an old revolver bought on the way, and his favorite sword-stick with an ivory-handle!

The Sunday after the Great War had commenced Riviere was staying the week-end at a house a few miles from Beaconsfield, and walked over to see the Chestertons. They were in a very

166

national state of excitement and emotion, as all were on such a day. His first thought was, what could he do to help his country,

"I couldn't wield a sword as I can't lift my right arm above my shoulder. I should be no use in cavalry, no horse could carry me." Then with a sudden hopefulness and that humor that was so often directed against himself, "I might possibly form part of a barricade."

The Chestertons, his brother Cecil, and his friend W. C. Worsdell, all belonged to a debating society known as "I. D. K." (I Don't Know). In the earlier period G. K. C. attended the meetings pretty regularly but later on rarely, being, as his wife declared, "too busy." One of the earliest meetings was at the Chiswick house, of his wife's family, the Bloggs. At the end of the discussion Chesterton remarked in his usual jocular style,

"We're in a complete fog!"

But more than once he declared that the speeches of the I Don't Knows were much cleverer than those heard in the House of Commons. At one meeting Chesterton could not find a chair, so he was obliged to squat on the floor, and he dropped down with a thud that shook the whole house!

One year the Chestertons were com-

167

ing back from Bromley after a delightful afternoon spent at E. W. Fordham's house where the guests had produced some plays written by their host—one of them an exceedingly clever and amusing take-off of G. K. C. himself which the original had greeted with continuous chuckles and gurgles of laughter. Having returned with them year after year from this show and knowing his habit, Riviere remarked,

"Aren't you going to have the usual cigar, Gilbert?"

"I was not going to have a cigar and I **don't** want a cigar, but if it's a case of a holy ritual here goes," he answered characteristically with a chuckle as he took out a cigar and commenced smoking.

While visiting Columbus, Ohio, to lecture, Chesterton had a friendly discussion with Professor Joseph Alexander Leighton and Dr. T. C. Mendenhall, the noted physicist—on the question whether veridical communications from the dead were received by living persons. Dr. Mendenhall contended that some at least of these communications were genuine, and therefore established the reality of life after death. Leighton took the role of skeptic, contending that when, as in some undoubted cases, bits of information, quotations, etcetera, had been received through mediums, they probably were due to subconscious memories, and that in other cases their apparent supernormal character was probably the result of coincidence. Chesterton agreed to the genuineness of the communications, but took the view that they were transmitted by bad spirits and that it was spiritually unhealthy for living persons to have any kind of traffic with them.

No one could condemn a thing in fewer words than Chesterton. Speaking about that much discussed book of other days, Renan's "Life of Christ," he said to his friends Desmond Gleeson and George Boyle,

"I remember reading it while I was standing in the queque waiting to see 'Charlie's Aunt.' But it is so obvious which is the better farce, for 'Charlie's Aunt' is still running."

The old English advertisement of "Charlie's Aunt" always had a picture of the old woman getting along at top speed, with the words, "still running."

Father Cyril Martindale did not meet Chesterton very often, but he felt that he knew him well all the same, "this was because despite his shyness, or I should say modesty, he let you know him, and intercepted no barriers. This modesty was again seen in his dealings with young men. It never occurred to him that they could have nothing interesting or useful to say, or that he was called upon to act the oracle.

"And this simplicity could again, I think, be seen in what people called his paradoxes. He always insisted that that was not what they were, but sheer statements of the obvious. To him, it was life as ordinarily lived that seemed 'paradoxical'—it was amazing to him that men could think the things they did, especially as doing so issued into so uncomfortable as well as, too often, so wicked a life.

"Sometimes the constant appearance of the word 'wild' in his writings irritated me. He had a vivid and active imagination, so that he saw all sorts of connections and illustrations that others did not: but his mind in reality worked in a very orderly way. I think the explanation may be this—he constantly described himself as 'lazy' and I expect that by temperament he was. He always put down the rapidity of his brother's conversion with the tardiness of his own, at sheer laziness on his part. Now had he let himself go to laziness, he would have been letting his mind, too, go 'wild.' But he did neither. Very likely he used the word in a slightly different sense from the one in which I used it: he felt it as the opposite of 'smug' and so forth. It remains that I think he had to conquer

170

a real tendency to laziness, and so, to letting his mind just hop about in a (to me) 'wild' and disorderly way.

"I think he died in some ways a broken-hearted man. There were no signs of the world having learnt anything that was good, even from its sufferings: all the more noticeable was his peace and serenity in God; and this is why I do not hesitate to say that I think there was to be discerned in him **real holiness**."

Father (now M o n s i g n o r) John O'Connor known to fame as Father Brown, recollects that on Sunday, July 30th, 1922, he had "the immense happiness of receiving Chesterton into the Church. Mrs. Chesterton was present, profoundly moved, and Dom Ignatius Rice, O. S. B., in the chapel of the Railway Hotel at Beaconsfield, the first public church in town. I remembered his lines written years before,

'Prince: Bayard would have smashed
    his sword
To see the sort of Knights you dub.
Will someone take me to a pub?
Is **that** the last of them? O Lord!
Will someone take me to a pub.?'

"In 1925 Mrs. Chesterton followed him into the Church on the Feast of All Saints. They almost at once began to sponsor the erection of a permanent

171

church near the railway station. **And** now it is being enlarged as a memorial to him.

"Gilbert Chesterton and I were wont to call down Mark Twain's name in benediction and to wish there were more like him, whether in his own States or any others. I recall many of our delighted exchanges on Mark the deathless. I was once thrilled to give him a patiche out of something he had not read,

" 'Buck Fanshaw's Funeral.'

"That he had not read it was to me a miracle. He had read everything I ever heard of that Mark Twain had written."

Patrick Braybrooke saw his cousin Chesterton for the last time at Beaconsfield. "It was a hot afternoon in summer and in the sweet garden at his home he recited poetry, made up verses, discussed American hotels, and came to the conclusion that Stevenson was the bravest man who ever wrote."

One morning not long afterwards as he was sitting in the refreshment room of a London underground, Braybrooke picked up casually enough a newspaper. "I saw some words and my world seemed to fall into pieces. For I read SUDDEN DEATH OF G. K. CHESTERTON. It seemed like the end of an era of literary greatness in every way.

172

But I was glad he did not have a long illness—a long drawn-out anti-climax was not for him. When his time came he went home quickly, almost as though like one of the Stevenson characters—hit by an arrow. He went home and the Catholic Church which he loved so well took care of his soul and in the little Church at Beaconsfield to the subdued mutters of the Mass we said our last farewell."

Chesterton died on June 14, 1936, and was buried in the graveyard of the Beaconsfield Catholic Church. Just recently the Republic of Ireland has given a great bell for the Chesterton Memorial Church thus inscribed.

"Presented to the parish of Beaconsfield by friends and admirers of Gilbert Keith Chesterton, to ring the call to faith, which he so chivalrously answered in song, in word, and in example, to the glory of God and of England."

Walter de la Mare penned a memorial quatrain to his life-long friend,

"Knight of the Holy Ghost, he goes his way,
Wisdom his motley, Truth his loving jest;
The mills of Satan keep his lance in play,
Pity and Innocence his heart at rest."

173

# INDEX

Page

Adams, James Truslow, meets Chesterton...78
Adams, Karl ..........................150
Aristotle .............................131
Armstrong, Prof. A. J., entertains C. .....58
Arnold, Matthew .....................127
Autobiography ........................145
"Ballad of the White Horse" ....94, 160, 162
Baltimore, liked by Chesterton .........128
Barnes, Bishop E. W., ..................108
Barr, Robert ..........................25
Barrie, James M. ......................37
Beaverbrook, Lord ....................108
Belloc, Hilaire ................. 7, 10, 14
    First meets Chesterton .............. 24
    Quoted ..................35, 44, 75, 133
Bent, Stephen Vincent ................162-3
Benet, William R. .....................158
Bentley, E. C. .................Iff., 5, 137
Bier ce, Ambrose ..................... 40
"Biography for Beginners" ..............85
Birkenhead, Lord .......... ....... 56, 109
Blackwood, Algernon ...................33
Blatchford, Robt. complimented by C.....21-3
Blessed Virgin ..................... 89-90
Blogg, Frances, marries C. ..............13
Boer War, opposed by C. ............19-20
Borden, Lucille ........................39
Boswell ........................... 7, 28
Bourne, Francis Cardinal ..............148
Braybrooke, Patrick, at C.'s funeral....172-3
Bridges, Horace J., debates with C.....68 ff.
Brown, Edw. tells of C.'s Welsh lecture 49-52
Browning, Robert.....3, 14, 58, 95, 125-6, 152
Cabell, James Branch ..................122
Carrell, R. Alexis, on C. ................123
Cecil, Lord ............................33
Cecil, Lord David ......................38
Cambridge ...........................107

175

# INDEX

Page

Canadian Authors' Society, toasted by C...76
Catholic Church, C. joins ...........90, 102
Chamberlain, Joseph ...................19
Chesterton, Cecil,, brother 14, 138-9, 167, 170
Chesterton, G. K. .....................
Chubb, T. C., describes C. at Yale......92-7
Clarke, Isabel C., entertains C. in Rome..35-6
Clemens, Samuel L. (Mark Twain ........19
    Praised by C. ...........135, 149, 172
Cobbett, William .................... 97-8
Columbus, Ohio, C. visits .............168
Connolly, Myles, impressions of C.......120
"Convert, The," poem by C. ............157
Cram, Ralph Adams ..........33 ff., 144 ff.
Eliot, T. S. ..........................146
"Everlasting Man" .....................118
Dante .................................153
Darrow, C., debates with C. ..66 ff., 117, 128
de la Mare, Walter, meets C. ....32-3, quoted
de Castro, Adolphe, meets C. ............40
Dickens, Charles, admired by C......3, 30, 95
"Pickwick Papers," C.'s favorite....131, 152
Distributism ....................... 14, 24
Drinkwater, John ....................51
Drood, Edwin .......................27-7
Doyle, Conan .........................117
Dudley, Owen F., meets C. ..............34
Duggan, Eileen ....................151 ff.
Dyboski, Roman ............... 132, 147 ff.
Falstaff .............................92
Father Brown .................25, 94, 144
Fletcher, James Gould ...............160-1
"Flying Inn, The" .............85, 95, 144
Fordham, E. W., boyhood friend ....4 ff., 168
France, Anatole .......................15
Frank, Waldo, admires C. ..............120
Frankeau, Gilbert, meets C. ...........25
Galsworthy, John, 24; discussed by C. ....129

176

# INDEX

Page

Garland, Hamlin, meets C. ..............119
George Fifth, King, meets C. ............11
Gibbs, A. Hamilton, meets C. ...........165
Gibbs, Sir Philip, meets C. ...........20-1
Gill, Eric, C.'s friend ..................27
Gilson, L. E. .....................149 ff.
"G. K.'s Weekly" .................. 14, 27
Glasgow, C. lectures in, 53; visits......165-6
"Goodbye, Mr. Chips," praised by C.......24
Gordon, Charles W., describes C. .........78
Graham, Cunninghame .................11
Graham, Kenneth, compared to C. ......35
"Greybeards at Play," C.'s first book .....14
Guedalla, Philip, meets C. ..............31-2
Gwynn, S,. recalls C.'s first book14, 17, 18, 38
Hamilton, Cosmo, debates with C. ....62 ff.
Hammond, J. L. ......................18-9
Hardy, Thomas ......................129
Harris, Frank ........................29
Hawthorne ..........................111
Henry Eighth, King .................36, 97
Hereford, Oliver, quoted ...............69
Hazlitt, Henry .......................117
Heine ...............................41
"Heretics" .................... 15, 30, 116
Hilton, James, writes C. as a boy ........23
Hirst, F. W., edits speaker with C. ........19
"History of England" ..................136
Holliday, Robert Cortes, meets C. ........127
Hollis, Christopher, meets C. ..............24
Holy Ghost ..........................95
Housman, A. E., 107; quoted by C.....129-130
Huxley, Aldous. admired by C. ..........63
"History of England" ..................136
Jackson, Holbrook, meets C. ..........41-45
Jacobs, W. W., meets C. ...............23
James, Henry ........................10
Joan of Arc, C. speaks on ..............33

177

# INDEX

Page

Johnson, Dr. Samuel 28, 36, 43, 88, 143, 165
    Chesterton dressed as ..............134
Kaye-Smith Sheila, praised by C........112
Kernahan, Coulson, meets C. ..........25-6-7
Kingsmill, Hugh, meets C. ..............29
Kipling, Rudyard ..............76, 96, 153
Knox, John .........................105
Lane, John ..........................15
Lenin .................................131
"Lepanto," poem by C. ........94, 119, 160
Lewis, Sinclair ................ 112-3, 127
Lindsay, Vachel .....................161
Liverpool, C. lectures in ................53
Locke, John .........................41
Lodge, Sir Oliver ......................21
Lowdnes, Mrs. Marie Belloc, meets C.......33
Mabbott, T. O., praises C. ............115-6
MacDonald, George ....................26
MacDonald, Ramsay ................26, 108
"Magic," play by C. .................116-7
"Man Who Was Thursday" .............. 3
    Praised by James Hilton ....24, 32, 95
    Admired by Mussolini .......134; 144
Martindale, Cyril C. ................167-171
Masefield, John .......................108
Masterman, Charles ....................11
May, J. Lewis ..........................15
Megroz, Rodolphe L., visits C. ............79
Miller, J. Corson .....................158
Moore, Tom ...................... 17, 18
More, Thomas .........................90
Mussolini, Benito, visited by C. ........134-5
Napoleon, quoted .....................120
"Napoleon of Notting Hill"—
      15, 16-7, 79, 85, 95, 116, 144
"New Jerusalem .......................87
"New Witness" ........................14
Notre Dame University, C. at ........99-113

**178**

# INDEX

Page

Noyes, Alfred .......................155-8
O'Connor, Father John ...........137-140
   Receives Chesterton Into Church...171-2
Oldershaw, J. L. ...................5, 18, 9
"Orthodoxy..........15, 32, 116, 149-50, 160
Ould, Hermon, offers C. club presidency..86
Oxford ...............................107
Patterson Mrs. F. T., hears C. lecture..66 ff.
Pearson, Hesketh ...............31, 140-1
Pemberton, Sir Max ...................143
Phelps, William Lyon .............98, 118
Philip the Second, misinterpreted by C.....119
Pollock, Channing ....................115
Poland .......................... 148 ff.
Quiller-Couch, Sir Arthur ...............51
Redfield, William C. ...................62
Remarque, Enrique Maria, C. dislikes ....64
Rinehart, Mary Roberts ................143
Ripley, Clements, admires C. ............32
Riviere, Hugo C., paints C. ............85-6
Roberts, R. Ellis, hears C. lecture ........46
Robinson, E. A. .................. 166, 197
Rodin ................................44
Rome, C. visits ............... 90, 97, 134
Rose, Sir Holland .....................107
Roseberry, Lord .. .................... 54
Ruskin, John ................... 19, 107
Russell, Bertrand, C.'s opinion of ......108
Russell, George ............... 98, 127-8
Sabatini, Rafael ................... 141-2
Saint Januarius .......................44
St. Louis, Missouri, C. lectures ....72-4, 128
Saint Paul's School ....................13
"Saint Thomas Aquinas" ..............150
Scott, Walter, 3; "Ivanhoe" reviewed by C...75
Shaw, Bernard, C.'s book on 15, 27, 44, 46, 55
   Meets Chesterton.. 75-6, 95, 96, 141, 146
Shorter, Clement K. ...................141

179

# INDEX

                                                   Page

Sheen, Fulton ...........................150
Slade Art School, attended by C. ........13
"Speaker," The ........................18-9
Stevenson, Robert Louis, quoted ..........83
Stewart, Bishop G. C., at C.'s lecture....68 ff.
Stewart, Donald Ogden, admires C. ......117
Strachey, Lytton, compared to C. ........35
Swinburne ............................... 3
Tennyson .......................... 3, 95
Thackeray .............................95
Thompson, Francis ....................155
Thomas, Edward ........................ 2
Thoreau, 111; quoted ..................121
Tinker, Chauncey B. ...................118
Titterton, W. R., C. writes ............81-3
     Describes C. ......................84
Tolstoy ..............................131
"Trent's Last Case," by E. C. Bentley ....137
Trevelyan, George M. ..................107
Trotsky ..............................131
Van Dine, S. S., admires Father Brown ...142
Van Druten, John ......................51
"Varied Types" ........................159
Velasquez ..............................44
"Victorian Age of English Literature" ...144
Walker, Headmaster, discovers C.'s genius.. 1
Walpole, Horace .......................132
Walsh, William Thomas, describes C...118-9
Watts, G. F., admired by C. ............ 3
"Well and the Shadows" ................146
Wells, H. G...34, 46, 64, 79-80-81, 86, 96; 133
West, Rebecca ........................109
Wise, Stephen S., admires C. ............122
Wood, Clement ........................161
Wright, Cuthbert ......................146
Wyndham, George ......................11
Yealy, Francis J., hears C. lecture .......47
Yeats, Elizabeth, at G. K.'s wedding ......13
Yeats, William B., 108; meets C. ......145-6

**180**